W9-DDH-785

THE FACE OF THE EARTH

Kevin Reilly, Series Editor

THE FACE OF EARTH
OF THE

ENVIRONMENT
AND
WORLD HISTORY

EDITED BY
J. DONALD HUGHES

M.E. Sharpe
Armonk, New York
London, England

Library of Congress Cataloging-in-Publication Data

The face of the earth: environment and world history / J. Donald Hughes, editor
p. cm. — (Sources and studies in world history)
Includes bibliographical references and index.
ISBN 0-7656-0422-1 (hc. : alk. paper)
1. History—Study and teaching. 2. Human ecology.
I. Hughes, J. Donald (Johnson Donald), 1932– . II. Series.
D16.25.F33   1999
907—dc21   98–55778
CIP

Printed in the United States of America

The paper used in this publication meets the minimum requirements of
American National Standard for Information Sciences—
Permanence of Paper for Printed Library Materials,
ANSI Z 39.48-1984.

BM (c)   10   9   8   7   6   5   4   3   2   1

Dedicated to
Robert E. Roeder
1931–1998
Founding member, World History Association
Professor of history, University of Denver
Colleague and friend

Contents

Foreword

The Face of the Earth: Environment and World History, the twentieth title in the series *Sources and Studies in World History,* inaugurates a minseries of collected essays on important topics in world history. Inspired in part by a conference of the World History Association, J. Donald Hughes, the editor of this first volume, has selected contributions from a wide range of environmental historians.

Environmental history is an ideal focus for world history. More than states, more than cultures or civilizations, environments are porous and pervasive; air and water and the seeds and germs they carry as passengers fill the world as if it were a vacuum. The atmosphere, the oceans, the resources of the earth form the only common legacy of world history.

Yet, the study of the environment places unusual demands on the historian. He or she must master specialized knowledge of biology, botany, geology, oceanography, and animal husbandry, to name but a few areas of expertise apparent in this volume. Another challenge is the need for a vantage point that allows him or her to appreciate and account for human action without ignoring its ecological context, trivializing the role of other natural forces, or celebrating exploitation.

Since Herodotus and Sima Qian, history has been the story of human exploits. Often, as Hughes reminds us here, world historians have shaped a narrative of human achievement that celebrated the victories of man over nature and applauded technological progress that often resulted in species depletion, soil erosion, river silting and salting, deforestation, or other forms of environmental degradation.

To reposition humankind in the context of the cosmos and fully acknowledge the consequences of human action require new sensitivities and a new vocabulary. We see both in the admirable essays presented here. John R. McNeill writes not only "Of Rats and Men," but of snails, sandalwood, whales, birds, mosquitoes, goats, and innumerable other "agents of all biological ranks."What we lack in knowledge of proper names and personal motivation is more than compensated by what we learn of the long-term ecological processes in the Pacific. Comparing Australian graziers and immigrant American cotton producers, Helen Wheatley shows each group with its own requirements and rewards but both "engaged in an intimate dialogue with nature."

The authors of these essays avoid the contrasting dangers of anthropomorphizing nature in order to make it humanity's obedient servant or of depriving the natural

world of all animation to render it mute before unalterable laws. The essays on the Pacific and Australia, along
with others on modern ecological thought in the United
States, Russia, and India, remind us that the health of the
planet is never a matter that can be left to chance or
scientific inevitability.

These diverse essays attest that there is no dogmatic consensus in environmental or world history, but together they
begin to define a field of study that may have the power to
brighten the face of the earth.

Kevin Reilly
Series Editor

Acknowledgments

As editor, I would like to thank several organizations and a number of individuals who have in various ways inspired this book and helped to bring about its creation. It was the World History Association (WHA), specifically its Rocky Mountain branch, that asked me to undertake the editorship and encouraged me at important points in the process. In particular, I would like to thank Heidi Roupp, Marilynn Jo Hitchins, and Frederick S. Allen, each of whom gave advice that proved to be indispensable in the process of putting the book together. I am also indebted to Jeanne T. Heidler, who served as program chair of the World History Association meeting on "The Environment in World History," at Aspen, Colorado, 8–10 October 1994, where several papers were presented that later became part of this book. The Aspen Institute and the Woodrow Wilson Foundation joined the WHA as co-sponsors of the conference, and their support is appreciated. Although this book is in no sense a conference proceedings, it was definitely inspired by the remarkable series of presentations and discussions that took place during those three spectacular autumn days in the Colorado Rockies. I am also grateful to Jerry H. Bentley of the *Journal of World History* for permission to print an abbreviated version of John R. McNeill's article "Of Rats and Men: An Environmental History of the Island Pacific."

I owe a debt of thanks to my colleagues in the American Society for Environmental History (ASEH). Several of them are authors of works in this collection. Hal K. Rothman, the editor of *Environmental History Review* (now *Environmental History*), gave me permission to use a major portion of my article "Ecology and Development as Narrative Themes of World History" as part of the introduction to this book. Special thanks go to John Opie, the society's first president and founding editor of the journal. The library of the Forest History Society, the ASEH's sister organization, gave access to its unparalleled collection of publications and manuscripts, for which I thank Michele A. Justice and Cheryl Oakes.

The University of Denver and its Department of History have supported this project with facilities and various forms of financial aid. In particular, I thank my chair, John Livingston, and his administrative assistant, Pat Reed. The amenities of the John Evans Professorship, kindly governed by William Zaranka, the university's provost, have made possible the time and effort I have been able to give to this editorship.

These acknowledgements would be incomplete without special thanks to my spouse, Pamela L. Hughes, who accompanied me to WHA on more than one occasion and has given me patient and generous support in my work.

THE FACE OF THE EARTH

1

J. Donald Hughes

Introduction

Ecological Process in World History

Development as the Organizing Principle
of World History

The organizing principle of virtually every world history text at present available and used in courses in North America is *development*.[1] The word occurs everywhere, often in such titles as *The Development of Civilization*.[2] The case for development is virtually never argued; it is simply accepted as an unquestioned good. The story, as usually told, takes humankind from one level of economic and social organization to the next in a nearly triumphal ascent. The account begins with a brief description of Palaeolithic hunters living lives that are nasty, brutish, and short. Then the agricultural revolution occurs,

Reprinted in part from *Environmental History Review* 19, no. 1 (Spring 1995): 1–16, © 1995 American Society for Environmental History. Reprinted by permission.

bringing a more dependable food supply. An even more important step comes with the urban revolution and origin of civilization. The Age of Bronze is an advance over the Age of Stone, and the Age of Iron and the Age of Steel follow. Every stage is portrayed as an improvement over what went before.

Many discussions of modern history assume that development is the desirable path for all nations. After World War II, the countries of the Third World were sometimes called "undeveloped" or "underdeveloped nations." These terms were later seen as pejorative and were replaced by "developing nations." The new term seemed more acceptable; although it still placed the countries behind the more developed world, it indicated that they were at least moving in the right direction. Although "development" is not defined, it can be inferred from the narrative to mean primarily economic growth and technological progress. World history texts describe achievements in the arts and sciences as well, but what they regard as a goal for the Third World is obviously not finer literature than Homer's, paintings that outdo Lascaux, or even discoveries in physics that will catch up with Einstein's. They regard it as the creation of factories, energy facilities, financial institutions, and the ever-increasing use of the Earth's resources for human purposes. They seldom consider the impact on the natural world that would occur if the rest of the world were to catch up with the industrial West, or whether sufficient natural resources to support such development exist. That is, the story line of development for the most part ignores the living and nonliving world. It has so far failed to address the issue of sustainability.

The Inadequacy of Development as an Organizing Principle

Development as an organizing principle of world history has produced a misleading account. The historical facts include many instances when development led to false starts and reverses, but world history texts leave these results out of the story or explain them as atypical exceptions. The disasters of development generally have occurred when ecological limits were ignored and exceeded, and the dominant modern story of world history either does not recognize or tends to deny the importance of ecological factors. Therefore, the story of world history as development does a disservice to the world community by failing to warn of dangers that should be evident from the accumulated experience of humankind.

History contains many instances of false starts and collapses of development that were environmentally related. The earliest known experiment with agriculture, which began between 15,000 and 12,000 B.C.E. in Egypt, ceased around 9,500 B.C.E., and there is no evidence of planted crops again until 5,200 B.C.E., when agriculture was reintroduced from Mesopotamia.[3] The hiatus is hard to explain, but climatic change seems a possible reason; this early attempt at agriculture may have failed because it was unable to adapt to environmental change.

Similarly, the first development of metallurgy in Europe, the copper industry of the Danube Valley in the fourth millennium B.C.E., flourished and then disappeared. Ruth Tringham believes that the smelters used immense amounts of wood, deforesting the landscape and destroying the fuel supply, and paleobotanical studies support her conclusion.[4] The environmental failure was brought about by human agency: development failed because the users of the new technology neglected to take steps to make it sustainable.

The urban revolution had its reverses, too. The early cities of the Indus Valley disappeared, and conquest does not appear to have been the cause.[5] There is evidence of flooding. In later levels at Mohenjo-Daro, brick is of poorer and poorer quality. The firing of millions of bricks over decades implies continuous consumption of major vegetation, and there was overgrazing as well. The land was bared, allowing runoff to swell rivers and cause flooding. The reduction of transpiration by forest trees desiccated the climate and altered rainfall patterns. Salinization, a hazard of irrigation in arid countries, was exacerbated by drying and the increased salt load from areas where forests had been removed. "Mohenjo-Daro was steadily wearing out its landscape, and being worn out in return."[6] Once again, development without environmental conservation could not be sustained.

Other examples abound, and they are not limited to the ancient world. How many world history texts come to grips with the role of deforestation and other forms of environmental deterioration in the crises of late medieval Europe?[7] The problem may be that authors absorbed in the narrative of development have failed to grasp the pertinence of the expanding literature of environmental history. They may not have read Alfred Crosby's *Columbian Exchange* or his more recent *Ecological Imperialism*[8] and thus have missed his radical biological retelling of the story of European expansion. To give another instance, they characteristically present the Great Depression as the result of financial imbalance only and do not consider that in North America, at least, it may have been "in a sense, a bill collector sent by nature."[9]

Some present trends run counter to faith in development. For example, the encroachment of humans into virtually every habitat on the planet has reduced the numbers of most other species, made many of them extinct, and seems unlikely to abate. A problem associated with encroachment on arid lands is salinization, which is a rapidly expanding threat. One way of coping with increasingly salty soils is to adapt halophytic plants to cultivation. But the development of naturally saline habitats for residential, industrial, and agricultural uses is on the verge of extirpating many halophytes that could become productive crops. One species of *Distichlis,* a salt-tolerant grain, has proved to be a viable food crop on saline land, but it was discovered only when it was almost extinct.[10] This is but one example of development almost preventing development; elsewhere it *has* prevented it.

The fact that development in the last days of the twentieth century threatens human survival through pollution of the atmosphere and waters, with the resultant destructive potentialities of acid precipitation, global warming, loss of the ozone layer, and the oxygen-generating capacity of the oceans, does not fit into the story line of world history as the triumph of development. The optimism expressed in world history texts is an extension of the momentum of the organizing principle of development. The wars and depressions of the twentieth century rendered more difficult the maintenance of a belief in "progress," but it has been replaced with development as a desideratum. Perhaps the two are not all that different; development is certainly less questioned, but it might be suspected that it is old progress writ large.

World historians did not invent the idea of development; they found it as a dominant concept in modern political economics, and it was and is important both in the theory of market capitalism and in socialism. But it is not the only available organizing principle. Even proponents of development recognize that, environmentally speaking, it is usually also destruction. For a nation to succeed in development would be for its natural resources to be used, for its forests to be turned into lumber and its coal and iron ore deposits into steel. In the process, the air would become more polluted and the rivers would become more laden with the products of erosion and waste. Environmentalists and developers alike recognize that to protect the environment is to curb development, and to develop is to degrade the environment. Human beings seem to want both goods, while recognizing their ultimate incompatibility. The first UN conference on the subject, held in Stockholm in 1972, was called the Conference on the Human Environment, but the second one, in 1992 in Rio de Janeiro, was deliberately renamed the United Nations Conference on Environment and Development so that no one should forget the necessity to consider the two principles together. As A.S. Bhalla remarked in his recent book, *Environment, Employment, and Development,* "The world has experienced unprecedented and spectacular economic growth since 1945, largely based on technological advances. However, the environmental impact of such development—reflected in increasing pollution, environmental deterioration, and the exhaustion of natural resources—has been a source of major concern, especially in the past twenty years, and this has led to increasing agreement that growth at such costs cannot be sustained for long, except at the risk of our own survival."[11] Recognizing that the international community is on the horns of a dilemma, world historians must look beyond development for an organizing principle.

Ecological Process as the Organizing Principle of World History

The new narrative of world history must have ecological process as its major theme. It must keep human events within the context where they really happen, and that is the ecosystem of the earth. The story of world history, if it is to be balanced and accurate, will inevitably consider the natural environment and the myriad ways in which it has both affected and been affected by human activities. Unlike some other organizing principles that world historians have adopted, the theme of the interaction of human events and nature has been operative during every chronological period. It modifies or determines all other organizing principles. Politics and economics ignore geography, geology, and biology to their peril, since the latter three reveal aspects of the order of things within which the former two operate, and on which they depend. People are animals who live as parts of regional ecosystems, and ultimately of the world ecosystem, and this fact determines what they may do without endangering their life support. Economics, trade, and world politics are regulated, whether humans wish it or not, and whether or not they are conscious of it, by the availability, location, and finite nature of what, in the language of development, are called "natural resources." A historian who has decided to place history within its context, and to "make ecological sense," will have to become an environmental historian.

Ecological process is a dynamic concept. It implies that the interrelationship of humans and the natural environment undergoes continual changes. These changes make environmental history just as necessary as ecological science in explaining the present predicament of humankind and nature. Past changes help to explain the present and lead us to expect further changes as history continues. The idea of balance as a desideratum in environmental history is too often taken as a search for a stagnant status quo. To counter this misunderstanding, the word *process* is added here. Balance is a useful concept in environmental theory, but it has several meanings. There is the static balance of a pyramid, in which every block is securely supported by those below. There is the unstable but compensatory balance of scales, in which a weight added to one side will cause the other side to go up, unless equal weight is also added there. And there is the living balance of a bird in flight, which compensates for variations in air currents by shifting the angles of its wings and tail. It is the balance represented by the last-mentioned metaphor accommodating change that ecological process implicitly seeks. Similarly, sustainability does not imply a static economy but one in which the use of resources varies with the capacity of the ecosystem to supply them without permanent damage. Environmental history describes an ecological process that has sometimes moved toward the balance and sustainability just described, but it has often moved away from them.

Too often, critics of environmental research have mistaken its concerns as an inappropriate nostalgia for some state of affairs in the past. There have certainly been environmentalists who have yearned for a simpler world.

Paul Shepard, in *The Tender Carnivore and the Sacred Game,* advised North Americans to return to a Palaeolithic way of life, although admittedly he would let them keep a few technological improvements.[12] But fortunately or unfortunately, like history itself, ecological process is irreversible. Human actions can divert, but cannot retrieve, time's arrow. Still, there is some hope of diverting it in a better direction, and that may prove to be one of the uses of environmental history.

The uncritical use of development as an organizing principle must be remedied. But if ecological process is adopted as the major narrative theme of world history, development will not disappear from the story; it will, however, need careful redefinition. Recent studies of economic growth in a world of limited resources have recognized the need for such revision. In *Beyond the Limits,* Donella and Dennis Meadows and Jørgen Randers quoted from a World Bank working paper:

> TO GROW means to increase in size by the assimilation or accretion of materials. TO DEVELOP means to expand or realize the potentialities of; to bring to a fuller, greater, or better state. When something grows it gets quantitatively bigger; when it develops it gets qualitatively better, or at least different. Quantitative growth and qualitative improvement follow different laws. Our planet develops over time without growing. Our economy, a subsystem of the finite and nongrowing earth, must eventually adapt to a similar pattern of development.

"We think there is no more important distinction to keep straight than that one," the authors continue. "It tells us that, although there are limits to growth, there need be no limits to development."[13] This meaning of development can provide an important interpretive function in the story of world history as ecological process. Development as economic growth that is unconscious of limits, and therefore is destructive of life as a whole, will no longer be regarded as a blessing. Mere growth in quantity, driven by an exponential expansion of human population, will collide with the limits of the Earth; indeed, it is doing so now. But development as improvement in quality; development as advancement in the fine arts and the arts of living; development as the discovery of ways to use resources more efficiently, more creatively, and not wastefully; development in moral inclusiveness—such development has a positive role. It can be directed in ways that conserve and are not destructive of Earth's biosphere.

Books on World History and the Environment

What teachers of the subject must demand is a world history that adopts ecological process as its organizing principle. The inclusion of an introductory chapter on the environment or the interpolation of sections dealing with environmental problems is inadequate. It is essential that world historians familiarize themselves with the work of environmental historians and keep the ecological context and the operation of environmental changes constantly in the forefront. As of this moment, a satisfactory world history of this kind has not appeared. Writers of world history in many instances have not even mentioned the destruction of the environment as they tell the story of the development of civilization. Giving attention to development while ignoring ecological process gives implicit approval to the environmentally destructive course of the modern world economy. Other writers, probably reflecting a desire on the part of a few publishers to respond to an evident demand for more information on environmental problems in world history, have tried to annex it to conventional approaches. Their attempts to include the environment as a popular subject, along with other relatively new, admittedly important themes such as the history of women and minorities, have generally amounted to nothing more than a tacking on of chapters and paragraphs that are not integrated with the main story line. These texts make a perfunctory bow in the direction of widespread contemporary environmental concern, but seem to regard the ecological crisis as a brief deviation in the ongoing story of human development that human cleverness and technology can rectify. Without acknowledging it, they subscribe to the idea of development as inevitable progress.

An effort to do more than this was Arnold Toynbee's *Mankind and Mother Earth,*[14] but it was unfinished at the time of the author's death, and it suffers from major flaws, the most important of which is an extremely cursory treatment of modern history. Despite a promising title and a prefatory section that takes ecology seriously, it remains for the most part a conventional political-cultural narrative that repeats observations made in Toynbee's earlier works. It can be appreciated as a gesture, however. Late in life, Toynbee apparently recognized that his *Study of History*[15] had failed to give ecological process the role it demanded, and the later book might be viewed as an incomplete and unsatisfactory attempt to remedy that defect. The landscape is still open for as many good historians as choose to paint it.

Three other books occur in this connection; they are presentations of environmental aspects of history, rather than attempts to narrate world history with the theme of ecological process, but they are worth reading and might provide supplemental reading in a course on world history. The best for college students, in spite of its technical style, is I.G. Simmons's *Changing the Face of the Earth: Culture, Environment, History.*[16] Written by a geographer, it takes a historical approach, sweeping from "primitive man" to "the Nuclear Age" with careful attention to questions of energy production and its environmental consequences. Population is given balanced and thoughtful treatment, and there are good photographs, charts, and maps.[17]

Another is W.M.S. Russell's *Man, Nature, and History,*[18] a brief, well-illustrated tour of world environmental history that is intended for secondary school readers but a book that might be read with profit by college students. It is a quarter of a century old, however, and does not deal with issues that have surfaced since then.

The most recent is Clive Ponting's *Green History of the World,*[19] a study of selected environmental issues through history. Although his style is journalistic and his sources undocumented and sometimes unreliable, Ponting's analysis is thoughtful, and his broad knowledge of the subject is impressive. The book, though not organized as a world history, deserves attention and might suggest some topics deserving of treatment in world history texts.

The Environment and World History

This book includes seven essays written by authors who take different approaches but share a conviction that world history writing must take ecological process seriously. Several of the authors are well-known scholars in environmental history, with fine publications to their credit. All the essays center on modern history, particularly the twentieth century, or treat it in an important way, although they may relate modern issues to their roots in earlier times. The modern world is different from the world before because the scale of our effects on the environment has passed a critical threshold. Economic growth, population growth, and the production of energy have increased so rapidly as to become revolutionary in their effects. At some point, a difference in the quantity of human impacts became a difference in quality. The topics of the pieces range from a sweeping view of the world as a whole, through regional studies that examine important aspects of human interrelationships with the global environment in various parts of the world, to a study of the influence of one important individual on his nation and beyond it.

My essay, which follows, traces the human relationship to biodiversity from the emergence of our species in dependence on biodiversity to the present time of the destruction of biodiversity. Even a treaty drafted by the United Nations in response to concern about the loss and exploitation of species defines biodiversity in terms of its economic value to nation-states.

The eminent urban environmental historian Martin V. Melosi contributes an essay that relates the themes of justice, race, and poverty to the environment. His study deals primarily with the environmental justice movement in the United States, but the issues raised in it are exactly those that characterize the dialogue between environmentalists in developing countries and those in industrial countries across the world.

John R. McNeill provides a synoptic study of a region vast in extent if relatively small in land area: the Island Pacific, which he delimits to embrace Melanesia, Micronesia, and Polynesia, including New Zealand. On those widely separated islands, evolution had produced a wide variety of relatively undisturbed ecosystems. The story of extinctions of native species, introduction of exotic animals and weeds, destruction of habitats and decimation of indigenous peoples was repeated on countless islands, perhaps showing in microcosm a process that occurred, and occurs, around the world.

The next three essays are centered in particular countries, discussing issues that have worldwide implications.

In "Land and Agriculture in Australia: Coping with Change in a Fragile Environment," Helen Wheatley describes the clash of two ways of viewing the landscape and treating the land: that of American cotton growers who emigrated to Australia in the 1960s, and that of the Australian sheep graziers they were replacing. Wheatley argues that the Americans brought in a capital-intensive technology that was integrated into the world market economy but out of touch with the local ecosystem. The graziers, although "creatures of empire" rather than "native sons of the soil," through bitter experience over generations had come to recognize "the true nature of the Australian interior and found the best way to exploit it."

Valery J. Cholakov offers a convincing demonstration that the Russian environmental movement, and the concerns that characterize it, did not arise during the upheavals of the 1980s and 1990s as a result of a new openness to Western influences but emerged from a long tradition of Russian thought about nature and attempts at conservation going back at least to the seventeenth century. Russian environmental views were not monolithic; from the time of Peter the Great onward, they were a subject of controversy between Westernizers, who sought some form of private and state conservation within a process of technological modernization, and Slavophiles, who felt a deep nationalistic value in the environment as a visible expression of Mother Russia. During the communist period, under Stalin and his successors, nature was overwhelmed by a series of "great transformations," and environmentalists who criticized governmental plans were repressed severely. With *glasnost* came a realization of the extent of environmental devastation, and although the green movements that emerged were dominated by political concerns, there are reasons to hope for a continued "eco-revival."

The final essay, by Diane M. Jones, portrays the extraordinary vigor of contemporary environmentalism in India and points to Gandhian thought as an important indigenous root. Although Gandhi himself seldom made direct mention of human relations to the natural world, his emphasis on simple living, self-sufficiency, and nonviolence and his opposition to economic exploitation and Western-style industrial development subsequently enabled environmentalists to regard him as an ally and predecessor. Recent environmental movements, such as the Chipko resistance to commercial deforestation, have used Gandhian methods and have included Gandhian leaders such as Sunderlal Bahuguna. Like Melosi, Jones recognizes an important connection between environmentalism and social justice. Jones notes that the connection is especially close in India and that it is part of the Gandhian heritage.

The author of each essay in this volume strives to understand how the process of human interaction with the natural environment unfolded in the past and to gain perspective on the ecological crises of the world at the beginning of the twenty-first century. The authors recognize the ways in which the living and nonliving systems of the Earth have influenced the course of human affairs. They evaluate the impacts of changes in human society as they relate to changes in the natural environment. In addition, they are interested in what people have thought about the natural environment, how people have expressed their ideas of nature, and how attitudes and concepts have affected human actions in regard to natural phenomena. Their shared conviction is that history today must be, as William Green put it, "perceptive of human interconnections in the world community," and at the same time just as discerning of "the interdependence of humans and other living beings on the planet."[20] The biosphere can no longer be seen as the stage setting on which human history is enacted. It is an actor; indeed, in a very real sense it provides a major portion of the cast.

Notes

1. The texts originally reviewed for this essay are, in chronological order, L.S. Stavrianos, *The World Since 1500: A Global History* (Englewood Cliffs, NJ: Prentice-Hall, 1966); J.M. Roberts, *History of the World:* vol. 1, *To 1500;* vol. 2, *Since 1500* (New York: Knopf, 1976); F. Roy Willis, *World Civilizations:* vol 1, *From Ancient Times through the Sixteenth Century;* vol. 2, *From the Sixteenth Century to the Contemporary Age* (Lexington, MA: D.C. Heath, 1982); Stanley Chodorow, Hans W.

Gatzke, and Conrad Schirokauer, *A History of the World* (San Diego: Harcourt Brace Jovanovich, 1986); Anthony Esler, *The Human Venture:* vol. 1, *The Great Enterprise: A World History to 1500;* vol. 2, *The Globe Encompassed: A World History Since 1500* (Englewood Cliffs, NJ: Prentice-Hall, 1986); Albert M. Craig et al., *The Heritage of World Civilizations* (New York: Macmillan, 1986); Peter N. Stearns, *World History: Patterns of Change and Continuity* (New York: Harper and Row, 1987); Robert W. Strayer et al., *The Making of the Modern World: Connected Histories, Divergent Paths (1500 to the Present)* (New York: St. Martin's, 1989); Kevin Reilly, *The West and the World: A History of Civilization,* 2 vols. (New York: Harper and Row, 1989); William H. McNeill, *A History of the Human Community: Prehistory to the Present* (Englewood Cliffs, NJ: Prentice-Hall, 1990); Jiu-Hwa L. Upshur, Janice J. Terry, James P. Holoka, Richard D. Goff, and Bullitt Lowry, *World History* (St. Paul: West, 1991); John P. McKay, Bennett D. Hill, and John Buckler, *A History of World Societies* (Boston: Houghton Mifflin, 1992); Peter N. Stearns, Michael Adas, and Stuart B. Schwartz, *World Civilizations: The Global Experience* (New York: HarperCollins, 1992); and Albert M. Craig, William A. Graham, Donald Kagan, Steven Ozment, and Frank M. Turner, *The Heritage of World Civilizations* (New York: Macmillan, 1994). It should be noted that some recent texts at the least have moved in the direction suggested here, among them the Reilly book listed above and Richard W. Bulliet et al., *The Earth and Its Peoples: A Global History* (Boston: Houghton Mifflin, 1997).

2. Harry J. Carroll Jr. et al., *The Development of Civilization: A Documentary History of Politics, Society, and Thought* (Chicago: Scott, Foresman, 1962), 2 vols., to give one example. It might be countered that the word is used innocently in a general sense, but for an analysis of the role of rhetoric, and the use of the word "development" in political discourse, see M. Jimmie Killingsworth and Jacqueline S. Palmer, *Ecospeak: Rhetoric and Environmental Politics in America* (Carbondale: Southern Illinois University Press, 1992), particularly p. 9, where "developmentalists" are defined as those "who seek short-term economic gain regardless of the long-term environmental costs."

3. Michael A. Hoffman, *Egypt Before the Pharaohs: The Prehistoric Foundations of Egyptian Civilization* (New York: Knopf, 1979), pp. 85–90.

4. Ruth Tringham, *Hunters, Fishers and Farmers of Eastern Europe, 6000–3000* B.C. (London: Hutchinson, 1971).

5. Robert Eric Mortimer Wheeler, *Civilizations of the Indus Valley*

and Beyond (New York: McGraw-Hill, 1972); Gregory L. Possehl, ed., *Harappan Civilization: A Contemporary Perspective* (Warminster, UK: Aris and Phillips, 1982); Gregory L. Possehl, ed., *Ancient Cities of the Indus* (Durham: Carolina Academic Press, 1979).

6. Wheeler, *Civilizations of the Indus Valley,* p. 72.

7. Charles R. Bowlus, "Ecological Crises in Fourteenth Century Europe," in *Historical Ecology: Essays on Environment and Social Change,* ed. Lester J. Bilsky (Port Washington, NY: Kennikat Press, 1980), pp. 86–99.

8. Alfred W. Crosby, *The Columbian Exchange: Biological and Cultural Consequences of 1492* (Westport, CT: Greenwood, 1972); and *Ecological Imperialism: The Biological Expansion of Europe, 900–1900* (Cambridge, UK: Cambridge University Press, 1986).

9. Stewart Udall, *The Quiet Crisis and the Next Generation* (Salt Lake City: Peregrine Smith Books, 1988), pp. 137–38.

10. Nicholas P. Yensen and Susana Bojorquez de Yensen, "Development of a Rare Halophyte Grain: Prospects for Reclamation of Salt-Ruined Lands," *Journal of the Washington Academy of Sciences* 77 (December 1987): 209–14.

11. A.S. Bhalla, *Environment, Employment, and Development* (Washington, DC: International Labor Office, 1992), p. 11.

12. Paul Shepard, *The Tender Carnivore and the Sacred Game* (New York: Scribner's, 1973).

13. Donella H. Meadows, Dennis L. Meadows, and Jørgen Randers, *Beyond the Limits: Confronting Global Collapse, Envisioning a Sustainable Future* (Post Mills, VT: Chelsea Green, 1992), p. xix; the quotation is from Robert Goodland, Herman Daly, and Salah El Serafy, *Environmentally Sustainable Economic Development: Building on Brundtland,* World Bank Environment Working Paper No. 46, July 1991, pp. 2–3.

14. Arnold Joseph Toynbee, *Mankind and Mother Earth: A Narrative History of the World* (New York: Oxford University Press, 1976).

15. Arnold Joseph Toynbee, *A Study of History,* 12 vols. (London: Oxford University Press, 1934–1961).

16. Ian Gordon Simmons, *Changing the Face of the Earth: Culture, Environment, History* (Oxford, UK: Basil Blackwell, 1989).

17. Ian Gordon Simmons, *Environmental History: A Concise Introduction* (Oxford, UK: Blackwell, 1993), is a brief, interpretative study of the principles involved in world environmental history.

18. William Moy Stratton Russell, *Man, Nature, and History: Controlling the Environment* (New York: Natural History Press for the American Museum of Natural History, 1969).

19. Clive Ponting, *A Green History of the World* (New York: St. Martin's, 1991).

20. William A. Green, "Environmental History," in *History, Historians, and the Dynamics of Change* (Westport, CT: Praeger, 1993), pp. 167–90.

2

J. Donald Hughes

Biodiversity in World History

We humans are not alone on the Earth. Our lives, our culture, our technology, and our art have been immeasurably enriched because our ancestors learned to watch, listen to, and imitate the other animals that share the land and sea with us. So the ancient Greek philosopher Democritus thought. He speculated that people learned how to weave from spiders and how to sing from songbirds, swans, and nightingales. Humans got the inspiration to build houses of clay from watching swallows at work on their nests. "In the most important concerns," he wrote, "we are pupils of the animals."[1] A more recent author, Steven Lonsdale, argued in a remarkable book filled with examples from every part of the world that dance owes its origin and development to human imitation of the varied movements of mammals, reptiles, amphibians, fish, birds, and even invertebrates.[2] The idea of the impacts of other forms of life on humans can be followed even further. Our species, from the earliest times down through history, gained more from other species than a few crafts. Interaction with countless kinds of animals and plants largely created the shapes of our bodies and minds, gave direction to human cultures, and in an important sense made us what we are. The diminishment or loss of that interaction has affected and will affect us more deeply than we commonly think.

Ecosystems and Humans

The human species and human culture evolved through interaction with entire communities of animals and plants. Of the two great influences that make humans what they are, heredity and environment, environment is undoubtedly the more powerful. After all, heredity itself encodes the results of millions of years of environmental influences on the human genome. Even genetic mutations are to some extent caused by environmental factors. Evolution is largely the result of natural selection that takes place because humans, during their history of development as a species, have been part of biotic communities in which their interactions with other species of animals and plants have decided whether or not they survived and reproduced.

One of the greatest mistakes made by modern urban humans, including the authors of textbooks on world history, is to think about themselves as existing and acting without reference to other forms of life. No species exists alone; every one relates to others in one or more of a number of

communities that ecologists like to call ecosystems.[3]
Ecosystems are groups of interacting organisms in particular environments, which recycle water, foods, and min-
erals in manifold ways. Energy flows through the system
from the primary producers, which are photosynthetic
plants, through a series of herbivores, carnivores, scavengers, and decomposers. Each species has its own niche
and preferred habitat within the ecosystem, a "job" and
an "address" that are created and limited in relation to
other species. The human species evolved in at least one
ecosystem, and historically it became adapted to several
of them. We could not exist without an ecosystem to
supply the necessary elements for life. All this is basic
ecology, but few world history texts make it an important
part of their narratives.[4]

Humans were formed by interaction with an exception-
ally rich and varied environment, along with countless other
forms of life. Anthropologists generally believe that the ecosystem within which humans first evolved was in East Africa. Although changes have occurred in every species, and
many species have become extinct, something like that early
ecosystem persists today in protected reserves in the Great
Rift Valley and the Serengeti Plain. It was, and is, an area
containing a variety of types of vegetation, often in proximity: swamps, dense riverine jungle, dry thorn forest, and
open savanna. This is what ecologists call *ecotonal* country.
Its inhabitants could pass quickly from grassland, say, to
forest, so early humans encountered hundreds of species of
plants. Even more impressive is the richness of animal life
in the region. Though much reduced today, the number of
species, as well as the numbers of individuals in those spe-

cies, is overwhelming. Herds of tens of thousands of zebras, wildebeests, various antelopes, and other herbivores migrate in search of the forage that suits them. Predators and scavengers are not far behind; the great cats, wild dogs, hyenas, jackals, and vultures assure that no flesh of fallen animals will remain for long. The surface of a lake is turned pink by hundreds of thousands of flamingos. These few images can only suggest the variety, complexity, danger, and stimulation faced by early humans, who hunted, gathered, dwelt, and served as prey in that nexus of constant interaction between species. The abundant and diverse interaction made us what we are. A large and subtle brain seems to have given some humans a survival advantage in dealing with a complex vegetation, devising tools, and outwitting herd animals and predators, so it seems that human intelligence is a response to the challenges offered by living among many other species. To quote Edward O. Wilson:

> How could it be otherwise? The brain evolved into its present form over a period of about two million years, from the time of *Homo habilis* to the late stone age of *Homo sapiens,* during which people existed in hunter-gatherer bands in intimate contact with the natural environment. Snakes mattered. The smell of water, the hum of a bee, the directional bend of a plant stalk mattered. . . . The glimpse of one small animal hidden in the grass could make the difference between eating and going hungry in the evening. And a sweet sense of horror, the shivery fascination with monsters and creeping forms that so delights us today even in the sterile hearts of the cities, could see you through to the next morning. Organisms are the natural stuff of metaphor and ritual. . . . The brain appears to have kept its old capacities, its channeled quickness. We stay alert and alive in the vanished forests of the world.[5]

Coevolution

During the course of history, human development has been deeply affected by relationships with other forms of life, so much so that it can be described as a process of complex coevolution, genetically and culturally. As humans became better hunters, animals became better at escaping them. If the bow and arrow were a response to the speed and caution of the prey, it seems equally likely that the deer that survived in the ancient forests tended to be more agile because they were the ones that had evaded the expert native hunters.[6]

Coevolution means that the development of each of two species is significantly affected by interaction with the other. An extreme example is symbiosis, such as that of the yucca plant and the yucca moth, neither of which could survive without the other; the plant is the moth's only food, and the moth is the plant's only pollinator. We have a similar symbiosis with some of our digestive bacteria. But *Homo sapiens* has experienced coevolution, both in a genetic and in a cultural sense, with a wide variety of species. Many of the most important cases of symbiosis in human experience resulted from domestication. World history texts too often portray the cultivation of plants and taming of animals as a one-sided process of conquest. It is not; in domestication, human behavior changed as much as, if not more than, than that of the domesticates. Theophrastus was in touch with this truth when he said, "If mankind is not the only living thing to which the term 'domesticated' is strictly appropriate, mankind is certainly the one to whom it most applies."[7] Dogs, the first domestic species, have altered because of our cultural selection of them. They are mostly friendlier and retain their puppylike characteristics longer than their vulpine ancestors, and breeding has given them many shapes, some fantastic, such as the Russian wolfhound and the Pekinese. But the event of domestication also altered the place of humans in the ecosystem and was in one sense an adaptation of humans to the pack structure.[8] When a dog lived with me, I altered my own behavior considerably to include a daily walk quite unlike one I might have taken by myself, and I gained a fascinating opportunity for learning the way another species senses the community of life. My dog was constantly relating to rich elements of the environment of which I was not always conscious, particularly other examples of *Canis familiaris,* present or absent. I cannot help noting that in another case of coevolution, cats seem to have changed less than the humans they allow to meet their needs. All domesticates change, and humans change, too. Domesticating wheat meant for humans a more sedentary life with permanent houses and pottery. Domesticating sheep and goats entailed for some an annual visit to mountain pastures.

Humans continued to interact with, and learn from, plants and animals, but domestication and later urbanization changed the attitude of humans toward the ecosystem. Human thought divided it into two realms, the wild and the cultivated. Earlier hunter-gatherers regarded other forms of life, whether predators, prey, or plants, as spirit beings, possessing power, worthy of respect, and capable of teaching arts, virtues, and higher truth. Animals were held to have spirit protectors, and these spirits, or the animals themselves, became gods. But for the Bronze Age peasant and city dweller, the wild and its inhabitants became enemies and game. The earliest Near Eastern epic poem, *Gilgamesh,* well illustrates this. When King Gilgamesh's rule in the city became oppressive, the gods created a wild rival or counterpart for him, a hairy man named Enkidu, who lived in the wilderness with the animals, running with them and warning them away from hunters' traps. Enkidu was a man among wild creatures, learning from them and protecting them. Then Gilgamesh sent a woman to seduce Enkidu. Besides sex, she offered him bread and wine, foods transformed from cultivated plants by human art. After that, the animals feared and fled from Enkidu, and he had to enter the city. The city wall or, more precisely, the line between the desert and the sown land, had become a barrier between humans and wild species. Animals not domesticated were extirpated, especially if they threatened humankind's crops and herds; Gilgamesh is portrayed killing lions because he saw them "glorying in life."[9] With that, hunting ceased to be the taking of the life of revered prey because of need. Hunting became sport.

Later, some Greek philosophers were bothered by the fact that humans kill and eat other organisms. A few, like Pythagoras, prohibited their followers from doing so, maintaining that animals and plants have souls like human beings.[10] Others, like Aristotle, justified their slaughter by denying that animals are rational. To the Stoics, the proof of this was that animals lack language. In the words of the British philosopher Richard Sorabji, "They don't have syntax, so we can eat them."[11] The Western tradition generally followed Aristotle and the Stoics.

War on the Wild

Over time, but especially in the past two centuries, human actions have greatly reduced the total number of species, and the number of individual organisms within most species, thus diminishing the complexity of ecosystems. This process began in the ancient world; the Indian epic *Mahabharata* records the burning of the great Khandava forest,[12] with every creature in it, as an offering to the fire god Agni. Krishna and Arjuna set the forest ablaze and guarded its edges, forcing back every animal that tried to escape. The Indian ecological historians Madhav Gadgil and Ramachandra Guha suggest that this mythological event preserves the memory of a real clearing by fire to displace hunters and gatherers, along with the forest ecosystem that had supported them, in favor of farmers.[13]

The grand mosaics in the Roman villa at Casale in Sicily show hunters and soldiers rounding up every imaginable large creature from tigers to ostriches for display and slaughter in the amphitheaters. In one great series of shows in honor of Trajan's conquest of Dacia, Roman *bestiarii* killed 11,000 wild animals. There was opposition even in earlier times; Cicero pitied the elephants he saw being killed in Pompey's show and refused to make the citizens of his province in Cilicia collect leopards for the games.[14] Juba II of Mauretania objected to the destruction of African wildlife by the Romans, and his son Ptolemy, grandson of Antony and Cleopatra, closed the arenas in Mauretania, shut down the animal port of Hippo, and enacted a conservation law to preserve animals.[15] These measures were ineffective; several species of animals, including elephant, rhinoceros, and zebra, became extinct in North Africa, and others declined. At the same time, Roman occupation of the region wiped out forests and initiated a process of desertification.

The destruction of wildlife continued in the medieval period. Hunters killed Britain's last native brown bear in the tenth century. Kings reserved forests for hunting, but killed thousands of animals. A single robe for Henry IV of England required 80 skins of ermine and 12,000 of squirrel. By 1526, the last British beaver had perished.[16] Elk, aurochs, and European bison diminished in number, as much because the expansion of agriculture restricted their habitats as from hunting. The woodland in much of Europe had been cleared during the twelfth and thirteenth centuries, and although the trees recaptured some territory after the Black Death, by the sixteenth century vast tracts had again been stripped completely of woods.[17]

In medieval times, the ancient idea that human beings can learn from animals survived in bestiaries, books that explained the supposed moral and religious meaning of various creatures. But these literary creations made almost no attempt to portray the actual ways of living things, and many of the beasts described, like the phoenix and unicorn, were imaginary.[18]

A major biological event beginning in the fifteenth century was the penetration of Europeans into virtually every part of the globe. This allowed them to encounter and be affected by plants and animals they had never seen before, but also to destroy them. Most importantly, Europeans did not travel alone; they took with them their domesticates and other species that came along, invited or not: food plants, weeds, animals such as pigs and goats, and disease organisms and rats, an assembly that has been called "portmanteau biota" by Alfred W. Crosby Jr. in his seminal books *The Columbian Exchange* and *Ecological Imperialism*.[19] It would seem that adding more species to newly discovered lands might have increased biological diversity, but in such places as the Americas, Australia, and almost all islands, the immigrants increased aggressively, and, aided by the slaughter of wildlife by the human invaders, they crowded out indigenous species and upset ecosystems. It was a process of enrichment, at least temporarily, for the Old World, which gained food species for humans and domestic animals, most prominently maize and potatoes. For humans and wild species in the new lands, it was a time of death.

In the early modern period, the dominant attitude toward animals and plants by Europeans and by most of the world since was economic materialism. Other species were viewed as commodities; the question of their rationality was hardly raised within the increasingly mechanistic worldview of the time. As Sir Francis Bacon expostulated, "The world is made for man, not man for the world."[20]

The Great Recessional

In the nineteenth and twentieth centuries, the process of destruction of other forms of life by humans escalated as the result of more powerful technology, an expanding exploitation of natural resources, and an increasing human population. In 1800, large sections of the continents were still wildernesses and teeming with wildlife. There seemed to be no end to the bounty of the sea. By the last decade of the twentieth century, extinctions had occurred on a scale matched only by catastrophic events of the geological record.[21] Whole species of fish that had been staples of the trade had vanished from the Atlantic Ocean, and the great whales were almost gone. Wildernesses on land shrank to isolated retreats, and none was safe from destructive invasions. Varieties of frogs and other amphibians mysteriously disappeared in many ecosystems around the world.[22] India had 4 million blackbuck antelope in 1800; only 25,000 are left. One of the blackbuck's major predators, the cheetah, has vanished from India. Similar declines have been recorded for other animals around the world. For the majority of ecosystems on Earth, these two centuries were the Age of the Great Recessional, as their areas shrank and their component species declined in number or died the ultimate death of extinction.

Learning from other living things took on a new character with the growth of modern science, particularly biology and medicine. Scientists discovered a great deal about species, and ecologists developed the concept of the ecosystem. Nevertheless, a genuine interest in describing species and learning their physiologies and ways of life in many instances involved acts of destruction in order to gain knowledge. Ornithologists shot birds in order to study and draw them. Until recently, almost all college biology curriculums required students to dissect frogs, often while the animals were still alive, and any students who refused might lose course credit. Sometimes major inroads were made into wild populations in the name of dissertations and research grants. A typical method of studying rainforest biodiversity is to fog a tree with insecticide, killing all the insects and then identifying and counting them. It is at least possible that this could make a species extinct just before it would have been first noted by science. What was apparently the oldest bristlecone pine tree in America, and possibly the oldest tree in the world, was cut down by a dendrochronologist who wanted to study its rings. The findings of science could be used to demonstrate the value of ecosystems and even to save some of them, but also to increase human power and domination.

Technology, originally invented as a series of responses to the challenges of other species, provided humans with immense power to fracture ecosystems and alter the environment. Assault weapons designed for horrible use in war came into the hands of poachers. In open-pit mines and elsewhere, bulldozers and excavating machines large enough to dwarf the dinosaurs stripped away whole landscapes. Giant dams controlled rivers, and their reservoirs flooded extensive lowlands that were home to many forms of life. The ancient forests fell to clear-cutting so rapidly as to threaten their total disappearance before the twenty-first century is half over. The unparalleled ecological richness of the Amazon rainforest, with the genetic record of millions of years of evolution and the potential knowledge that might come from its study, began to give way to unsustainable agricultural and grazing projects of questionable long-term value. In an essay of this length it is possible only to mention the horrors of chemical and radioactive pollution that has poisoned life over millions of acres and has been detected even in the snows of Greenland and the bodies of Antarctic penguins.

The driving force in the recessional of other forms of life was the pressure of growing human population. Most of this increase has occurred during the twentieth century. In each of the past few years, the human population of the Earth has increased by over 90 million. This is a figure equal to at least 130 percent of the total population of the Roman Empire at its height. Nearly 90 percent of this increase was in the so-called Third World, and most of these people will be poor by the standards of the so-called developed nations. An increased number of people demands more land for agriculture. Many of them hunt, poach in reserves, fish, and collect animals to sell, not because they want to, but because other means of support for them and their families are not available. Supposing that economic improvement were possible for them, they will demand television sets, VCRs, automobiles, and houses with air conditioning. The free market will not, of itself, preserve the world's biodiversity. It only assures that the rarest products, whether they be rhinoceros horn, bear gall bladders, or elephant ivory, will rise in price to the point where it remains economical to import them. Democracy will not, of itself, assure the survival of nature reserves and endangered species in conditions of overpopulation. Around the world, people have encroached on reserves, and governments that want their support have failed to protect natural habitats.

The Biodiversity Crisis

In considering the environment's impact on humans in terms of interaction with other species, it seems clear that in the past century or two, the tables have been turned. At present, humans are making an unprecedented impact on the environment. This has given many people a sense of unease. There is a feeling at large that nature will have the last impact, and it is unclear just what it will be. In recent years, a crisis of biodiversity has been recognized by scientists, writers, and the international community. Anyone who doubts that need only try a computer word search for "biodiversity" among the titles in recent publications. The last time I did it, I found over 550, and this for a word that only recently appeared in dictionaries. But the tenor of international discussions of the question is not entirely encouraging for the survival of natural ecosystems.

When environmental questions first appeared on the agenda of international bodies, that of the survival and welfare of other species was prominent among them. The constitution of the first environmental organization under UN auspices, the International Union for the Protection of Nature, in 1949 defined its purpose as "the preservation of the entire world biotic community."[23] This organization became the International Union for the Conservation of Nature and Natural Resources (IUCN) in 1956. It undertook a survey of threatened animals which became the basis of the Red Data Book, the recognized international list of endangered species, first issued in 1960. Realistically but ominously, this was a loose-leaf book, allowing the insertion of additional pages. It now includes plants as well as animals. A cooperating organization, the World Wildlife Fund, founded in 1960, supported projects to preserve wildlife and their habitats in many nations.

UNESCO sponsored a Biosphere Conference in Paris in 1968 that discussed the human impact on the Earth's ecosystems and called for a major effort of research and education. An outgrowth of this conference was the Man and the Biosphere Program (MAB), with study of "the interrelationships between natural ecosystems and socio-economic processes" as one of its main aims.[24] By 1982, MAB had initiated 1,030 field research projects involving over 10,000 researchers in seventy-nine countries. Its International Coordinating Council evolved the idea of biosphere reserves as representative samples of significant ecosystems, and habitats of plants and animals including rare and endangered species. This is an international network of areas that would assist in the maintenance of biodiversity, and in 1979, there were 208 reserves in fifty-eight nations. A key principle of biosphere reserves is the establishment of buffer zones in which traditional uses are encouraged, thus working to assure the support of local communities.

The landmark international environmental meeting of the century convened in Stockholm in 1972: the United Nations Conference on the Human Environment, which included representatives of 113 nations, 19 intergovernmental agencies, and 400 nongovernmental organizations (NGOs).[25] The meeting was held at a time when the news that acid precipitation was causing the death of forests and aquatic life in many countries, and the subject of the loss of biological diversity understandably received attention. The most notable achievement of the Stockholm Conference, however, was the creation of the United Nations Environment Programme (UNEP), with its headquarters in Kenya, a Third World country. UNEP cooperated with other agencies, negotiating international agreements such as the Convention on International Trade in Endangered Species of Wild Fauna and Flora (CITES), the Bonn Convention on Migratory Species, and a whaling moratorium.

In the two decades after Stockholm, a number of important

issues involving ecosystems received world attention. Perhaps foremost among them was the rapid destruction of major portions of the tropical rainforests. Scientists pointed out that rainforests were living communities that included the vast majority of animal and plant species on Earth and that their removal would mean a crisis of extinction. Between the mid-1970s and mid-1980s, the timber extracted legally from the primeval forests of the Brazilian Amazon rose more than 270 percent, from 10.36 to 28.10 million cubic meters.[26] In addition, entrepreneurs and settlers cut and burned much larger amounts to open land for grazing and cultivation, activities that in many instances were not sustainable. By 1980, according to the UN Food and Agriculture Organization, 78 percent of Ghana's forests had been logged, and Costa Rica was cutting 4 percent of its forests annually.[27] When a single ridge top in Peru was cleared, more than ninety plant species known only from that locality were lost.[28] A group of women in India began a movement called Chipko that actively opposed the cutting of trees on the watersheds above their villages by talking to the laborers and putting their bodies next to the trees, and won a moratorium.[29] At the same time, the original forests of giant trees in the northwestern United States and western Canada, and the vast taiga of the Soviet Union, were, if anything, being logged faster than the Amazon.

In the United States, Congress had enacted laws to protect endangered species in 1966 and 1969. The spotted owl, which nests only in the ancient forests, was classified as threatened in 1988. Court orders forced a halt to logging those forests until a compromise could be worked out that would protect enough forest to enable the bird to survive. It would be better to frame the issue not around a single species but around the survival of the ancient forest ecosystem with its myriad interacting species. But there is not yet a law to protect endangered ecosystems. In the late 1960s and 1970s, international concern often appeared over the danger to single species: the panda in China; the tiger in India and Siberia; and the elephant in Africa, whose numbers crashed disastrously as a result of ivory poaching. These are highly visible indicator species, but the real problem in each case is the diminishment of the ecosystem to which each of them belongs. It is a process often called "habitat destruction," but it is really the fragmentation of communities of life.

One of the main arguments used for the preservation of ancient forests was that they are vast storehouses of species producing substances that might prove to be of use to humankind as medicines or in other ways. This is certainly true; researchers derived many healing drugs from tropical rainforests, and recently taxol, a derivative of the yew tree, a species once destroyed by loggers as a useless "weed," proved itself valuable in treating ovarian cancer. Biodiversity, the world suddenly realized, had economic value, and the discussion changed its tenor.

In 1987, a commission chaired by Prime Minister Gro Harlem Bruntland of Norway issued a report, *Our Common Future,* that recommended a second immense world conference on ecological and economic problems. The United Nations approved the idea, and the UN Conference on Environment and Development (UNCED), often called the Earth Summit because so many heads of state attended, met in Rio de Janeiro during June 1992, on the twentieth anniversary of the Stockholm conference. Incidentally, during the twelve days of the conference, humans removed 2,160 square miles of forest and took 6 billion pounds of fish from the oceans, and erosion carried away 792 million tons of topsoil.[30] Biodiversity was one of the major topics on the agenda at Rio, and the Convention on Biological Diversity was one of five primary documents that emerged from the conference. The UN Environment Programme (UNEP) had called for such a treaty and had convened working meetings in the four years immediately preceding the summit meeting.[31] The vast weight of discussion, however, was not on the need to preserve species and ecosystems, but on the desirability of assuring sustainable economic development for the nations of the world, and to distribute equitably the gains realized from the development of biological resources. The goals of the treaty expressed in the final draft are the conservation and sustainable use of biodiversity and fair trade and compensation involving products made from the genetic resources of nations. It charges each country to make plans to protect habitats and species and provides for aid to developing countries to help them do this. There are financial arrangements governing the use and sharing of benefits and the regulation of biotechnology. The treaty was signed by 153 nations of the 178 attending; only the United States voiced a refusal to sign, chiefly on grounds that the financial obligations were open-ended and insufficiently supervised. Since then, administrations have changed, the U.S. president has signed the treaty, and at this writing it awaits ratification by the Senate.

The emerging international consensus on biodiversity raises several questions. It assumes that the other forms of life on earth are the property and under control of nation-states. It specifically forbids interference in the way any nation chooses to protect or exploit the species within its borders. Yet national frontiers rarely coincide with ecosystems, and the welfare of life on the whole planet is obviously of concern to all. Some of the NGOs that attended the Global Forum parallel to the Earth Summit perceived a certain narrowness at the governmental level and drafted alternative treaties that attempted to express that concern. For example, the alternative Forest Treaty states, "The structure, function, and integrity of ecosystems must be seen to have infinite value. Every form of forest life is unique and requires adequate habitat and protection."[32] But most of the alternative treaties attempt to address other economic and cultural issues. At the conference, 178 nations and almost 8,000 NGOs sent representatives, but no other species had representation, nor did any ecosystem.

Response

If the most significant aspect of the environment's impact on humans has been the formative influence of living within ecosystems on genetics and culture, it is worth asking what effect living in a world of declining and disappearing species and diminishing ecosystems has and will have in the future. Human beings coevolved along with other species within communities of life, but now those communities are losing their complexity as they shrink in area and relinquish many of the forms of life that were members of them. It can be inferred that the changes in relationships to other species are exerting evolutionary forces on the human species and altering not only the quality of life but human nature itself.

It is interesting to speculate what the response of the human species might be to this challenge. The challenge is serious because *Homo sapiens* is not immune to the threat of extinction through degradation of essential supporting ecosystems. A real danger derives from the modern tendency to treat the natural world, not as a series of ecosystems that include human beings, but as a set of resources and commodities separate from humankind. Living forests are conceived as economic abstractions, which means clear-cutting to save on labor costs, not careful selective silviculture. A farm in traditional agriculture, such as that of a Balinese rice farmer, had to be treated as a whole, and therefore as a community of life. In Bali, plants that elsewhere are regarded as weeds turn up on the table as delicious cooked vegetables, and insects in the paddies are controlled by flocks of domestic ducks. In contrast, agribusinesses in these days of the so-called Green Revolution use immense inputs of pesticides, herbicides, and fertilizer to achieve monoculture with higher output but of questionable sustainability. The subsidy the economy has been taking from wild nature may be near an end,[33] as the last wild places yield to the inexorable advance of tree farms, industrial agriculture, strip mines, power plants, and urban encroachment. Pollution carried by air and water to formerly distant regions affects even protected wilderness. When the last natural ecosystems are in small, carefully protected reserves, many humans will certainly feel a sense of loss and of being closed in. When most wild species are extinct or survive only in captivity, not a few people will feel lonely and less free.

Many will not be conscious of this particular deprivation,

even though they suffer from it. In 1800, only about 2.5 percent of the world's population lived in cities. By 1985, the proportion in cities was more than 40 percent, and in the twenty-first century, more than half of all humans will live in large urban concentrations. Third World cities are growing most rapidly, and their slums make up much of this growth. For most city dwellers, the experience of other living species is limited to pets and a few opportunistic species that flourish in the urban environment, such as rats, pigeons, cockroaches, and the scavenging kites that one sees flying above cities in India, searching for food.

The evolution of the human species is at a turning point. If the cultural attitudes of the modern industrial age remain the determiners of human actions in regard to the ecosystems of which humans are part, while the human population continues to increase or remains at its present excessive level, an unprecedented crisis of survival is certain in the new century, whose beginning occupies the collective mind. But students of history know that massive cultural and economic changes have occurred before. Anyone who reflects on the altered certainties of the period from 1987 to 1994 would hesitate simply to extrapolate the trends of the twentieth century into the twenty-first. Humankind is subject to change as a result of the impact of a rapidly diminishing biosphere. Our culture is malleable, and will alter in unpredictable ways. Our thoughts and words shift from day to day. Even our genome is changing.

It is interesting to speculate what kinds of changes might reflect an adaptation of humankind to the threatened loss of forms and communities of life:

1. One would be a fall in the birthrate, undoubtedly. This is already occurring, but not rapidly enough to avert the crisis.
2. A worldwide trend toward reinhabitation, where local people take responsibility for protecting their own ecosystems, would be one of the most positive signs.
3. A sustainable agriculture and a forestry that assures the survival of the forest community are absolutely necessary.
4. Preservation of examples of undisturbed ecosystems in biosphere reserves would aid in the restoration of other areas.
5. More pressure on governments by movements opposing the destruction of nature, like India's Chipko, would be a positive sign.
6. One of the most effective trends would be wider education of children and adults in the facts of ecological and reproductive responsibility. Incidentally, this should include world history classes that include study of human interactions with the environment in every area and period.
7. Already visible is the beginning of a revival within religions of traditions that teach respect and stewardship for all creatures great and small. It is important to emphasize that this means not only kindness to individual animals but preservation of their habitats and of the integrity of creation.

We must learn to think of ourselves not only as humans but as forms of life, since that is what we are. As Edward Wilson put it, "We are in the fullest sense a biological species and will find little ultimate meaning apart from the remainder of life."[34] The community of life itself, in its many forms, and not humankind alone, made us what we are and is what we must in turn foster and protect. The most effective way to learn this is to observe and listen to the great council of all the beings that share the Earth with us.

Notes

1. Democritus fr. 154. See Philip Wheelwright, *The Presocratics* (New York: Odyssey Press, 1966), p. 184.

2. Steven Lonsdale, *Animals and the Origin of Dance* (London: Thames and Hudson, 1981).

3. See Frank Benjamin Golley, *A History of the Ecosystem Concept in Ecology: More Than the Sum of the Parts* (New Haven: Yale University Press, 1993).

4. See the recommendations in the Introduction.

5. Edward O. Wilson, *Biophilia* (Cambridge: Harvard University Press, 1984), p. 101.

6. J. Donald Hughes, *North American Indian Ecology* (El Paso: Texas Western Press, 1996), p. 4.

7. Theophrastus *De Historia Plantarum* 1.3.6. This is the author's translation.

8. Stephen Budiansky, "The Ancient Contract," *U. S. News and World Report,* March 20, 1989, pp. 74–79.

9. N.K. Sandars, trans., *The Epic of Gilgamesh* (Harmondsworth, UK: Penguin Books, 1960), p. 94.

10. J. Donald Hughes, "The Environmental Ethics of the Pythagoreans," *Environmental Ethics* 2 (Fall 1980): 195–213.

11. Richard Sorabji, *Animal Minds and Human Morals: The Origins of the Western Debate* (Ithaca, NY: Cornell University Press, 1993), p. 2.

12. Believed to be on the site of the modern city of New Delhi.

13. Madhav Gadgil and Ramachandra Guha, *This Fissured Land: An Ecological History of India* (Berkeley: University of California Press, 1993), p. 79.

14. Cicero *Letters to Friends* 7.1.3.

15. Dio Cassius 39.38.2–4; Pliny *Natural History* 8.7. 20–21.

16. Peter Verney, *Animals in Peril* (Provo, UT: Brigham Young University Press, 1979), pp. 40–41.

17. Charles R. Bowlus, "Ecological Crises in Fourteenth Century Europe," *Historical Ecology: Essays on Environment and Social Change,* ed. Lester J. Bilsky (Port Washington, NY: Kennikat, National University Publications, 1980), pp. 86–99.

18. Florence McCulloch, *Medieval Latin and French Bestiaries* (Chapel Hill: University of North Carolina Press, 1960), pp. 15–17.

19. Alfred W. Crosby Jr., *The Columbian Exchange: Biological and Cultural Consequences of 1492* (Westport, CT: Greenwood Press, 1972); and *Ecological Imperialism: The Biological Expansion of Europe, 900–1900* (Cambridge, UK: Cambridge University Press, 1986).

20. Donald Worster, *The Wealth of Nature* (Oxford, UK: Oxford University Press, 1993), p. 212.

21. Edward O. Wilson, *The Diversity of Life* (Cambridge: Harvard University Press, 1992), p. 32. See also Paul and Anne Ehrlich, *Extinction: The Causes and Consequences of the Disappearance of Species* (New York: Random House, 1981).

22. Kathryn Phillips, *Tracking the Vanishing Frogs: An Ecological Mystery* (New York: St. Martin's, 1994).

23. John McCormick, *Reclaiming Paradise: The Global Environmental Movement* (Bloomington: Indiana University Press, 1989), p. 38.

24. UNESCO, *Backgrounder: The MAB Programme* (Paris: UNESCO, 1982), p. 3.

25. McCormick, *Reclaiming Paradise,* p. 97.

26. Michael J. Eden, *Ecology and Land Management in Amazonia* (London: Belhaven, 1990), p. 94.

27. Judith Gradwohl and Russell Greenberg, *Saving the Tropical Forests* (London: Earthscan Publications, 1988), p. 36.

28. Edward O. Wilson, "Threats to Biodiversity," *Managing Planet Earth: Readings from Scientific American Magazine,* ed. Jonathan Piel et al. (New York: W.H. Freeman, 1990), p. 56.

29. Vandana Shiva, *Staying Alive: Women, Ecology and Development* (London: Zed Books, 1989), pp. 67–77.

30. Adam Rogers, *The Earth Summit: A Planetary Reckoning* (Los Angeles: Global View, 1993), pp. 19–20.

31. Edward A. Parson, Peter M. Haas, and Marc A. Levy, "A Summary of the Major Documents Signed at the Earth Summit and the

Global Forum," *Environment* 34, no. 8 (October 1992): 14.

32. Rogers, *Earth Summit*, p. 269.

33. For this apt metaphor, the author is indebted to a fine analytical study by Anthony B. Anderson, Peter H. May, and Michael J. Balick, *The Subsidy from Nature: Palm Forests, Peasantry, and Development on an Amazon Frontier* (New York: Columbia University Press, 1991).

34. Wilson, *Biophilia*, p. 81.

3

Martin V. Melosi

Equity, Eco-Racism, and the Environmental Justice Movement

According to historian Clayton R. Koppes, the American conservation movement took "its distinctive political form" during the Progressive era. Three ideas dominated: efficiency (management of natural resources), equity (distribution of the development of resources rather than control by the few), and aesthetics (the preservation of nature free from development).[1]

It is not surprising that of the three ideas, efficiency held the greatest sway. In the late nineteenth and early twentieth centuries, the nation was engaged in the relentless pursuit of economic growth. Supporters of the "gospel of efficiency"—proponents of applied science and environmental management—did not want to undermine development per se but questioned short-term private gain at the expense of long-term public benefit. Although this view was not wildly popular among all capitalists, or would-be capitalists, it certainly was less threatening than strict preservationism.[2]

Koppes argues further that for many conservationists of the Progressive era, "efficiency was not enough; they were also concerned for greater equity." In this context, "equity" implies that natural resources remain in public control so that their benefits could be distributed fairly. "The equity school," Koppes stateS, "saw wise use of the environment as a tool to foster grass-roots democracy."[3]

I have argued elsewhere that "wise use" was not a tool for equity but a "happy compromise" for government officials, who began to realize that they faced a potential contradiction in promoting economic growth, on the one hand, and providing stewardship over the public lands, on the other. The wise-use concept provided a middle ground to support sustained economic growth.[4] In either case, efficiency, not equity or Aesthetics, dominated Progressive era America and beyond.[5]

By the 1960s, according to Koppes, the efficiency school remained dominant, the aesthetic school at least had successfully protected the national park and monument system, but the equity branch wallowed. Without grassroots organizations to press for change—and with resistance to redistributive efforts at every turn—equity moved little beyond the conceptual stage.[6]

The emergence of the Environmental Justice Movement in the late 1970s offers a tantalizing opportunity to ask whether "environmental equity" has at last found its place in the modern American environmental movement (although this issue has potential implications for other places, especially the Third World). And also to query what constitutes environmental equity or environmental justice as advocated by its most recent proponents.

It is significant that the Environmental Justice Movement does not view itself as an outgrowth of the more traditional, or mainstream, American environmental movement. Its members and leaders openly disclaim common roots, objectives, and agendas. In October 1991, a multiracial group of more than 600 met in Washington, D.C., for the first National People of Color Environmental Leadership Summit. In its state of Principles of Environmental Justice, conference participants asserted the hope "to begin to build a national and international movement of all peoples of color to fight the destruction and taking of our lands and communities" resting on the reestablishment of "our spiritual interdependence on the sacredness of our Mother Earth," and, among other goals, "to secure our political, economic and cultural liberation that has been denied for over 500 years of colonization and oppression, resulting in the poisoning of our communities and land and the genocide of our peoples."[7]

For the most part, the movement has found its strength at the grassroots, especially among low-income people of color, who faced serious environmental threats from myriad toxics and hazardous wastes. According to sociologist Andrew Szasz, "The issue of toxic, hazardous industrial wastes has been arguably the most dynamic environmental issue of the past two decades." By 1980, "the American public feared toxic waste as much as it feared nuclear power after Three Mile Island."[8]

The reaction of local groups to toxics (such as lead poisoning or exposure to pesticides) and to hazardous wastes may have begun as NIMBYism (Not in My Backyard) but has evolved into something much different. Lois Marie Gibbs of the Citizens Clearinghouse for Hazardous Wastes stated, "Our movement started as Not In My Backyard (NIMBY) but quickly turned into Not In Anyone's Backyard (NIABY) which includes Mexico and other less developed countries."[9]

What has emerged, according to Szasz, is a radical environmental populism—ecopopulism—within the larger tradition of American radicalism, rather than an outgrowth of the modern environmental movement. By one estimate, almost 4,700 local groups appeared by 1988 to oppose toxics. Before the publicity over Love Canal (1978), contact between the groups was scant, but into the 1980s a more vibrant and better networked social movement appeared to be emerging.[10] Some scholars argue that the struggle for environmental justice for people of color may predate the 1970s, but these earlier efforts generally were contested under the rubric of "social" as opposed to "environmental" problems.[11]

For those articulating the goals of the movement, grassroots resistance to environmental threats is simply the reaction to more fundamental injustices brought on by long-term economic and social trends. According to Cynthia Hamilton, associate professor of Pan African Studies at California State University, Los Angeles, the consequences of industrialization "have forced an increasing number of African Americans to become environmentalists. This is particularly the case for those who live in central cities where they are overburdened with the residue, debris, and decay of industrial production."[12] In some instances, the critique extends to a questioning of the capitalist system, private property, and Eurocentric social viewpoints.

For some in the movement, especially African Americans and other people of color, the struggles against "environmental injustice" are, as sociologist Robert D. Bullard noted, "not unlike the civil rights battles waged to dismantle the legacy of Jim Crow in Selma, Montgomery, Birmingham, and some of the 'Up South' communities in New York, Boston, Philadelphia, Chicago, and Los Angeles."[13] "The environmental justice frame," stated sociologist Stella M. Capek, "is built around a concept of rights constructed in part by the actions and rhetoric of previous social justice movements. Most notable among these is the civil rights movement."[14]

Within this context, activists in the movement are claiming a full range of rights for any social group, including fair public treatment, legal protection and compensation. Bunyan Bryant and Paul Mohai of the School of Natural Resources at the University of Michigan have taken the argument a step further, contending that the civil rights movement, which faltered in the late 1970s and 1980s, may be seeing its resurgence in the area of environmental justice.[15]

The Environmental Justice Movement, therefore, is intentionally characterized as having its historic roots in civil rights activism but not in conservationism or the more recent environmental movement. It appears that this distinction emerged out of a desire to maintain a separate, albeit unique, identity for the sake of the movement's political objectives and to eschew what it perceives as the antithetic goals of mainstream environmental groups.

Mainstream environmentalism, especially as represented

by the so-called Group of Ten or Big Ten,[16] is characterized by those in the Environmental Justice Movement as
white, often male, middle and upper class, primarily concerned with wilderness preservation and conservation, and
insensitive to, or at least ill-equipped to deal with, the interests of minorities. Token representation of people of color
in mainstream organizations, especially in positions of authority or on the staffs, is an additional reminder of the gap
between the movements.[17]

In its most strident form, criticism of mainstream environmentalism includes charges of racism. For instance,
black activist Cliff Boxley, an unsuccessful candidate for a
seat on the San Mateo County Board of Supervisors in
1980, spoke out against "green bigotry." A more common
charge against mainstream environmentalists is that they
view human needs and interests as subservient to animals,
trees, and waterways. "Conservationists," Boxley charged,
"are more interested in saving the habitats of birds than in
the construction of low-income housing."[18] Bryant and
Mohai concluded:

> [Environmentalists] are viewed with suspicion by people of
> color, particularly as national environmental organizations try
> to fashion an urban agenda in the 1990s. To champion old
> growth forests or the protection of the snail darter or the habi-
> tat of spotted owls without championing clean safe urban en-
> vironments or improved habitats of the homeless, does not
> bode well for future relations between environmentalists and
> people of color, and with the poor.[19]

There is a division of opinion within the Environmental
Justice Movement, nonetheless, over whether to join forces

with mainstream environmental groups, to cooperate with them in areas of common interest, or simply to follow a separate path in order to achieve its goals. Politics always makes strange bedfellows.

Among people of color, however, criticism of mainstream environmentalism is not meant to leave the impression that minorities have little or no concern for a full range of environmental issues, although this impression is widespread. A survey published by a graduate student at Michigan State University in 1973 came to the conclusion that blacks were not as interested in ecology as whites, largely because they felt alienated from many of the main currents in American life.[20] This view has been echoed by environmentalists over the years. In a 1990 issue of *Earth Island Journal*, Carl Anthony, an African American and president of Earth Island Institute, observed, "African Americans could benefit from expanding their vision to include greater environmental awareness." He went on to suggest that young African American males in particular face "utter alienation" from the natural environment and that "the loss of this contact with living and growing things, even rudimentary knowledge of where food and water come from, must present serious consequences that we, as yet, have no way of measuring."[21] But as Paul Mohai argued also in a 1990 study, "although blacks and other minorities appear to be disproportionately burdened by [environmental] hazards, little is known about the extent of awareness, concern, and political activity of these groups regarding environmental quality issues."[22]

To counteract the assumption that people of color lack an interest in the environment, supporters of the Environmental

Justice Movement have attempted to broaden discussion of the issue. Dana A. Alston, director of the Environment, Community Development and Race Project of the Panos Institute in Washington, D.C., attempted to place environmentalism in a larger social context. "Communities of color have often taken a more holistic approach than the mainstream environmental movement, integrating 'environmental' concerns into a broader agenda that emphasizes social, racial and economic justice."[23] In an effort to dispel the notion of environmental advocacy as "a white thing," several studies point to the strong environmental voting record of the congressional Black Caucus and the commitment of minorities to clean-air and clean-water legislation.[24]

In analyzing the evolution of the environmental movement, sociologist Dorceta E. Taylor pointed to greater "niche space partitioning" in recent decades to explain the diversity of groups and their choice of issues existing under the single umbrella of environmentalism. But she added that existing environmental groups have largely failed to attract minorities as a result of the appeals and incentives they promote. For instance, the argument that minorities are struggling to meet basic needs and thus place environmental issues low on a list of priorities assumes that the priorities are permanently fixed. According to Taylor:

> The argument does not allow for the possibility that environmental issues could become high-priority issues for minorities by redefining environmental issues in terms of basic needs, or that individuals might seek to meet high-order needs before all of their basic needs are met. Because many of the environmental problems facing minorities are immediate and life-

threatening, it is predicted that they will become involved in environmental organizations and groups, if and when these groups deal with issues of survival and basic needs.[25]

Various grassroots organizations seem to have met that criterion. In analyzing several studies conducted in the 1970s and 1980s concerning the different levels of black/white involvement in environmental issues, Taylor concluded that the environmental "concern gap" between blacks and whites can be understood by exploring the disparity between "concern" and "action." First, previous studies may mask levels of black concern because of measurement errors, either inappropriate indicators and/or poor sampling techniques.[26] Second, blacks have a history of higher rates of affiliation with voluntary social, political, or religious associations than whites.[27]

A most persuasive argument about the relationship between people of color and environmental concern/action is the notion that environment is a cultural construct, and participation in issues must be understood from that perspective. Barbara Deutsch Lynch's study of Latino environmental discourses sheds light on contrasting views of the environment between U.S. Latino peoples and Anglo-American environmentalists. The study took into account the role of "the garden and the sea" as traditional sources of livelihood for Spanish-speaking people—as well as instruments of bondage to dominant economic systems such as plantation life—and contrasted these perceptions with such images as the frontier, wild rivers, and forests in the Anglo-American community. "The ideal or utopian natural landscapes of Latino writers," Lynch observed, "are peopled and productive." Lynch also explored other questions of nature, homeland, ethnicity, and the idea of Indians as environmental guardians. She concluded that by "looking at the impact of environmental ills or mitigation programs on U.S. Latinos solely in terms of end points determined by Anglo environmental agendas (siting of toxic waste facilities, for example) only perpetuates the silence of Latino voices on the environment and postpones fundamental changes in the U.S. environmental discourse."[28]

The assertions of an existing, if sometimes masked, set of environmental interests among people of color and the characterization of the mainstream environmental movement as elitist and narrow in its vision suggest a description of minority grassroots environmentalism given by law professors Regina Austin and Michael Schill: "anti-bourgeois, anti-racist, class conscious, populist, and participatory."[29]

Environmental racism, not surprisingly, has become the central concern of the Environmental Justice Movement. Some in the movement connect class and race, but many others view racism as the prime culprit. Reverend Benjamin F. Chavis Jr., former head of the NAACP, is credited with coining the term "environmental racism" during his tenure (1985–1993) as executive director of the United Church of Christ's Commission for Racial Justice (CRJ).[30] Others, however, such as sociologist Robert Bullard, have been exploring the issue of environmental racism since the late 1970s.[31]

The Reverend Chavis became interested in the connection between race and pollution in 1982 when residents of Warren County, North Carolina—a predominantly African American area—asked the CRJ for help in resisting the siting of a PCB (polychlorinated biphenyl) dump in their community. The protest proved unsuccessful, resulting in the arrest of more than 500 people, including Chavis, Dr. Joseph Lowery of the Southern Christian Leadership Conference, and Congressman Walter Fauntroy of Washington.

The Warren County incident and others—some affecting middle-class blacks as well as the poor—convinced Chavis and his colleagues that a national study correlating race and toxic-waste dumping was in order. After five years of work, the CRJ produced *Toxic Wastes and Race in the United States: A National Report on the Racial and Social-Economic Characteristics of Communities with Hazardous Waste Sites* (1987). Under the research direction of Charles Lee, the report was the first comprehensive national study of the demographic patterns associated with the location of hazardous waste sites. The findings stressed that the racial composition of a community was the single variable best able to predict the siting of commercial hazardous waste facilities in a community. Minorities, especially African Americans and Latinos, were overrepresented in communities with these facilities. Moreover, the report concluded, it is "virtually impossible" that these facilities were distributed by chance, and thus race must play a central role in location. Supporters of the report's findings argued that other, less comprehensive studies conducted as far back as the 1970s generally corroborate the findings.[32]

The CRJ report, especially its strong inference of deliberate targeting of communities because of race, gave powerful ammunition to those interested in broadening a concern over ill-defined "environmental equity" into the Environmental Justice Movement. Recent statements by

Reverend Chavis, for example, demonstrate the broadening and the fleshing out of the call for environmental justice:

> Millions of African Americans, Latinos, Asians, Pacific Islanders, and Native Americans are trapped in polluted environments because of their race and color. Inhabitants of these communities are exposed to greater health and environmental risks than is the general population. Clearly, all Americans do not have the same opportunities to breathe clean air, drink clean water, enjoy clean parks and playgrounds, or work in a clean, safe environment.
>
> People of color bear the brunt of the nation's pollution problem.[33]

This is also true with respect to Chavis's more recent, all-exclusive definition of environmental racism:

> Environmental racism is racial discrimination in environmental policymaking. It is racial discrimination in the enforcement of regulations and laws. It is racial discrimination in the deliberate targeting of communities of color for toxic waste disposal and the siting of polluting industries. It is racial discrimination in the official sanctioning of the life-threatening presence of poisons and pollutants in communities of color. And, it is racial discrimination in the history of excluding people of color from the mainstream environmental groups, decision making boards, commissions, and regulatory bodies.[34]

At the extremes of the movement, there are those who view "environmental racism" as insufficiently descriptive of existing circumstances, proffering terms such as "American apartheid" or "toxic colonialism" with respect to dumping hazardous materials in Third World countries. Some consider dumping on Indian reservation sites as "environmental genocide." No matter what the term, the civil rights abuses of the past—slavery, indentured servitude, segregation—are meant to be clearly linked to the present environmental problems.[35]

The question of deliberately targeting communities of racial and ethnic minorities is viewed by some leaders of the movement as indispensable in keeping the focus on the relationship between race and pollution. PIBBY (Place in Black's Backyard) is seen as replacing NIMBY. Also critical are efforts to reject the notion that siting decisions are most often based on distinction by class, not race. Noting examples in Houston and elsewhere, Bullard has argued that "since affluent, middle-income, and poor African Americans live within close proximity of one another, the question of environmental justice can hardly be reduced to a poverty issue."[36] And even if companies are placing polluting technologies and industries into minority communities with their approval, "job blackmail" is viewed simply as racism of a different sort with similar consequences.

The perceived culprit in deliberate targeting is not simply private companies but also government. "In many instances," Bullard asserted, "government is the problem." He argued that a "dominant environmental protection paradigm" has been in operation that, among other things, institutionalizes unequal enforcement of laws and regulations, favors polluting industries over "victims," and delays cleanups.[37]

Efforts by the federal government to address some of the concerns over environmental racism, injustice, and inequity have been viewed with skepticism by those within the Environmental Justice Movement. A June 1992 report issued by the Environmental Protection Agency (EPA), *Environ-*

mental Equity: Reducing Risk for All Communities, supported some of the claims of the exposure of racial minorities to high levels of pollution, but it linked race and class together in most cases. Bullard viewed the study as an attempt "to mount a public relations campaign to drive a wedge between grassroots environmental justice activists and mainstream civil rights and environmental groups rather than offer[ing] a substantive effort to address environmental problems that disproportionately harm people of color and low-income citizens."[38] A study conducted by the *National Law Journal* in 1992 questioned the EPA's environmental equity record, pointing out that in the administering of the Superfund program disparities exist in dealing with hazardous waste sites in minority communities compared with white neighborhoods. William Reilly, EPA director under Presidents Reagan and Bush, was strongly criticized by movement members for not attending the People of Color Environmental Summit. And despite convincing President Clinton to sign an *Executive Order on Federal Actions to Address Environmental Justice in Minority Populations and Low-Income Populations* to "focus Federal attention on the environmental and human health conditions in minority communities and low-income communities with the goal of achieving environmental justice," there is disappointment because an Environmental Justice Act has yet to pass Congress.[39]

If we are to accept Andrew Szasz's view that the Environmental Justice Movement is the spearhead for a radical environmental populism that has the potential to transform the modern environmental movement, then it would be useful to assess the viability of its message and its relationship vis-à-vis mainstream environmentalism.

There is little doubt that the Environmental Justice Movement has reintroduced, and in many ways broadened, the issue of "equity" as it relates to environmentalism. The movement has persuaded—or possibly forced—environmental groups, government, and the private sector to consider the importance of race and class as a central feature of environmental concern for Americans as well as for people of color in the Third World. It has helped to elevate the toxics and hazardous waste issue to a position of central importance among a vast array of environmental problems. It has shifted attention to urban blight, public health, and urban living conditions to a greater degree than earlier efforts by environmental reformers. And it has questioned the demands for economic growth at the expense of human welfare. Whether or not the Environmental Justice Movement grows beyond its current strength, it has altered, and could possibly transform, the debate over the goals and objectives of environmental policy in the United States.

The movement, however, is not without its limitations. Its stance is sometimes inconsistent on the issue of race versus class; it can underestimate its friends and sometimes mischaracterize its foes; and it bears its own exclusivity. After all, the Environmental Justice Movement, although born at the grassroots, is a political movement with an agenda that questions many traditional practices and values and attempts to define new ones.

The core view that race is at the heart of environmental injustice is born of some persuasive evidence and an intellectual and emotional attachment to the civil rights heritage of the past several decades. Few, including the EPA, would deny that poor people of color are often disproportionately impacted by some forms of pollution. But the qualifiers are significant. Outside the movement, there has been serious questioning: Is the issue environmental racism or poverty? Even within the movement, there are those who cannot separate race and class in all instances. And to appeal to a broader constituency, given the political goals of the movement, it may be unwise to do so.

Michel Gelobter, an assistant commissioner for Policy and Planning for the New York City Department of Environmental Protection, has examined the connection between environmental regulation and discriminatory outcomes. In his studies of exposure to air pollution (total suspended particulates) in urban areas between 1970 and 1984, he concluded that there were some inequities in average exposure by race and small differences by income. In comparing relative improvements in air quality in those years, however, he found that the poor experienced a much lower relative decrease in exposure than the rich, while nonwhites experienced slightly greater relative reductions than whites.[40] Such findings point to the complexity of the issue of race, class, and environment, especially when different forms of pollution are measured. Air pollution is particularly difficult to evaluate because of its often ubiquitous nature—in, for example, ambient sources such as auto emissions—which fails to discriminate between rich or poor, black or white. Several forms of water pollution are equally ubiquitous.

Most of the attempts to measure pollution and relate it to distribution have been conducted by economists. Leonard P. Gianessi, Henry M. Peskin, and Edward Wolff produced the first study that examined the distribution of pollution on a nationwide basis. They were concerned with government efforts in the 1970s to apply uniform regulations over the entire nation:

> Although the theory of efficient environmental management suggests that the degree of control should reflect local geography and tastes, pressures for uniformity have been brought to bear by local political leaders who are afraid of losing industries to areas with less stringent controls. Thus, there is a clear bias in existing laws toward technologically defined and fixed standards that limit the allowable emissions of a polluter regardless of where he is located.[41]

The study concluded that when the distribution of policy benefits are considered with the distribution of costs of pollution abatement, the results are not uniform. It indicated, however, that lower-income groups gain the most in this instance, with nonwhites (except those in the highest-income group) leading the way.[42] Given the difficulty in utilizing all appropriate indicators, this study must be viewed as producing incomplete and inconsistent results. If it had examined more than air pollution, especially some kinds of land pollution, the conclusions might have been more concrete. Yet, by moving beyond anecdotal evidence and intuitive conclusions, Gianessi, Peskin, and Wolff demonstrated the difficulty in determining a conclusive pattern that links race to incidence of pollution.

Even with the widely disseminated study of the Commission for Racial Justice, questions have arisen about the efficacy of its conclusions concerning race. Gelobter discussed one of the study's key findings—that approximately 24 percent of minorities have one hazardous waste facility in their zip-code area, although they represent only 12 percent of the population. "But because minorities make up approximately 24 percent of the urban population of the United States," he wrote, "it's possible that most hazardous waste sites are simply in urban areas." "This study's measure of environmental discrimination," he concluded, "would have been strengthened if it had controlled for urban- versus rural-located facilities."[43]

Vicki Been, a law professor, also had reservations about the report. While she stated that there was significant evidence of disproportionate siting of the locally undesirable land uses (LULUs), "sufficient to require legislatures to address the fairness of the distribution of LULUs," she maintained that the evidence "does not establish that the siting process, rather than market forces such as residential mobility, caused the disparity"; "does not establish that siting decisions intentionally discriminated against people of color or the poor"; and "is limited by the imprecision of the study's definition of the neighborhoods compared."[44] The mobility issue is critical, for example, because white neighborhoods with polluting industries that eventually are populated with minorities cannot necessarily be considered "targeted" with respect to race. In future studies, terms such as "minority community," "African American neighborhood," and so forth, need to be defined more clearly. Distinctions between "inner cities versus suburbs" with respect to environmental risk also need to be recast in order to reflect current definitions of urban growth and development. Metropolitan areas especially are a complex of multiple cores, peripheral development, and edge cities. In cities such as Houston, for example, "inner city and suburb" does not sufficiently explain the geographic distribution of the races. African American and Latino enclaves exist throughout the metropolitan area and are not confined to a single core at the center of the city. Such a perception misrepresents the nature of modern cities and ascribes to "suburbia" concepts that are long outdated.

The issue of intentional placement of environmental risks in minority neighborhoods or communities—deliberate targeting—also is a knotty problem and is clearly the most controversial charge made by those in the Environmental Justice Movement. While anecdotal evidence exists for such practices, uncovering a consistent pattern of behavior or documenting such a racially motivated policy is very difficult.

Often cited as an example of deliberate targeting is the so-called Cerrell report. In 1984 the California Waste Management Board commissioned Cerrell Associates to advise the state on how to deal with political impediments to siting mass-burn incinerators. The confidential report concluded that the state was likely to meet less resistance in a low-income, blue-collar community than in a middle- or upper-class area. While the report helped confirm the existence of targeting practices by class, race was not a category in Cerrell's demographic analysis.[45]

A significant impediment to making the case for deliberate targeting is the lack of judicial remedies. In the broadest sense, civil rights law approaches are difficult when attempting to prove deliberate targeting. At this time, no court ruling has clearly supported claims of civil rights violations in selecting sites for polluting operations. In *Bean* v. *Southwestern Waste Management Corp.* (1979), the first lawsuit of its kind, a class-action suit was filed against the city of Houston, the state of Texas, and Browning Ferris Industries for the decision to site a municipal landfill in Northwood Manor (a middle-income neighborhood whose populatuib is 82 percent African American). The plaintiffs claimed that the decision was in part motivated by racial discrimination. The court ruled that the decision was "insensitive and illogical" but that the plaintiffs had not demonstrated the intent to discriminate on the basis of race. Similar suits faced the same result.[46]

Legal experts recognize the current lack of legal remedies and have suggested alternatives. Alice Brown of the NAACP Legal Defense and Educational Fund in New York City recommended utilizing environmental and public health laws, rather than civil rights law, to achieve the same ends. Others suggest avoiding abstract calls for fair siting and utilizing instead specific theories of fairness. And still others recognize the value in seeking a federal equity mandate through legislation, an effort that has been mounted in the past few years without success.[47]

The limited findings in available studies on race, class, and environmental risks, and the difficulties in proving deliberate targeting, not only suggest the need for more research but bring into question whether the insistence on race (separate from class) as the key variable in exposure to environmental risk is a wise tactic within the Environmental Justice Movement. Is the movement painting itself into a corner? The political value of such a claim is potent, but for greater credibility, the connection of race with class may prove to be a stronger position to defend.

The equivocal relationship with mainstream environmentalism also blurs the positioning of the Environmental Justice Movement in terms of its stance on environmental issues. Clearly, there is much to justify the criticism of the mainstream environmental groups for failure to include people of color and low-income groups into their ranks. Frederick D. Krupp, executive director of the Environmental Defense Fund, noted, "The truth is that environmental groups have done a miserable job of reaching out to minorities."[48] And there is reason to believe that the priorities of the "Big Ten" often have been focused on wilderness protection, preservation, and outdoor recreation at the expense of some urban-based problems.

In other respects, however, some in the Environmental Justice Movement have often mischaracterized mainstream environmentalism to the same extent that they themselves have either been marginalized or ignored by the major environmental groups. The evolution of modern environmentalist thinking and action suggests that there is much common ground with those involved in grassroots protests, including minorities.

While old-style conservationists focused on efficiency, aesthetics, and a small dose of equity, the modern environmental movement has been involved not only in natural environment issues, such as outdoor recreation, wildlands, and open space, but in concerns over environmental pollution and the maturing of ecological science. Environmentalists generally share an appreciation for the fragility of ecological balances, a notion of the intrinsic value of nature, a personal concern for health and fitness, and a commitment to self-reliance. Many, if not all, of these values can be found in the Principles of Environmental Justice articulated at the People of Color Environmental Summit. In addition, the politics of so-called mainstream environmentalists vary more sharply than their critics claim. They by no means espouse uniform political views or reform tactics. Some accept governmental intervention as a way to allocate resources or preserve wildlands and natural habitats. Others are suspicious of any large institution as the protector of the environment. Some believe that the existing political and social structure is capable of balancing environmental protection and economic productivity. Still others blame capitalism for promoting uncontrolled economic growth, materialism, the squandering of resources, and even the coopting of the environmental movement for its own ends. Aggressive, often militant, protest and citizen action have been carried out by groups such as Greenpeace, Friends of the Earth, Zero Population Growth, the National Wildlife Federation, Ecology Action, and a host of grassroots antinuclear organizations.[49] Mainstream environmentalists also give attention to urban issues through attention to pollution abatement and public health problems, but not to the extent that the Environmental Justice Movement has made urban environmental problems a centerpiece of their program.[50]

Some members of both movements (or both parts of a larger movement) have already begun to seek common ground to form alliances or sponsor joint ventures. Some major groups, for example, have attempted to establish an Environmental Consortium for Minority Outreach in Washington, D.C., especially after Benjamin Chavis and others openly protested the lack of minority representation on their staffs.[51] Yet much remains to be done to bridge the gap in a divided environmental community.

Critics of the environmental movement, from the right as well as the left, always have attempted to present it as monolithic, out of touch with the realities of everyday life. The variety of views and objectives within the broad environmental community cannot be so easily characterized, nor can its values be distilled into a homogenous belief system. Likewise, the depths and nuances of minority environmental views have not and will not be so easily gauged. Real accommodation between the various elements in the environmental movement will need to come down to a more concerted effort to understand and appreciate the variety and depth of a host of values and agendas.

The Environmental Justice Movement, despite its controversial stances on race, class, and the environment and its skepticism of the goals and objectives of mainstream environmentalism, is playing a historic role in reintroducing "equity" into public and academic debate over environmental policy. And this is an issue not confined to the United States. The Third World faces questions of environmental justice not only with respect to its own internal affairs but as a result of pressures from the outside, especially as a potential dumping ground for toxics and hazardous wastes from developed countries.[52]

Equity has been transformed into "environmental justice," with a particular focus on the traditional American underside caught under the wheels of an avaricious economy. In evaluating the nature of environmental movements through the 1970s, sociologist Allan Schnaiberg argued that the redistributive element (such as a windfall profit fund to provide cost offsets to the poor) has been largely absent from most of the history of environmental movements, "despite rhetorics that have been vaguely populist" and that environmental movements "are simply not welfare-oriented to the degree that a stable sustained coalition-building effort will be possible."[53]

The Environmental Justice Movement is welfare oriented and action oriented. Many in it will tell its critics that to question studies pointing to the correlation between race and environmental risk is to miss the point. Robert Bullard expressed that view when he wrote that "environmental scientists have not refined their research methodologies to assess the cumulative and synergistic effects of all of society's poisons on the human body. However, some health problems cannot wait for the tools to catch up with common sense."[54] There likely are many in the movement who share economist A. Myron Freeman III's observation: "It seems to me that the problem is not so much finding out more about the equity implications of possible policy alternatives, but getting the political system to come to grips with them and resolve them."[55]

It is this impatience that defines the Environmental Justice Movement today—for better or for worse. Impatience with the status quo has brought its message of equity, justice and eco-racism to public and academic attention, but impatience may also limit its appeal if it cannot convince enough people of the rightness of its cause. As Austin and Schill have argued, "Pollution is no longer accepted as an unalterable consequence of living in the 'bottom' . . . by those on the bottom of the status hierarchy."[56]

Notes

1. Clayton R. Koppes, "Efficiency, Equity, Esthetics: Shifting Themes in American Conservation," in *The Ends of the Earth: Per-*

spectives on *Modern Environmental History,* ed. Donald Worster (New York: Cambridge University Press, 1988), pp. 233–34.

2. The most important study on Progressive era efficiency in particular and conservation in general is Samuel Hays, *Conservation and the Gospel of Efficiency: The Progressive Conservation Movement, 1890–1920* (Cambridge: Harvard University Press, 1959).

3. Koppes, "Efficiency, Equity, Esthetics," pp. 235–36.

4. Martin V. Melosi, "Energy and Environment in the United States: The Era of Fossil Fuels," *Environmental (History) Review* 11 (Fall 1987): 167–68.

5. Koppes stated that the creation of the National Park Service in 1916 was the chief political victory of the aesthetic wing, but such a victory was wrought with contradictions. Natural resources were preserved, but public access to them threatened to destroy preservation. Koppes, "Efficiency, Equity, Esthetics," pp. 237–38.

6. Ibid., p. 251.

7. Quoted in Karl Grossman, "The People of Color Environmental Summit," in *Unequal Protection: Environmental Justice and Communities of Color,* ed. Robert D. Bullard (San Francisco: Sierra Club Books, 1994), p. 272.

8. Andrew Szasz, *Ecopopulism: Toxic Waste and the Movement for Environmental Justice* (Minneapolis: Minnesota University Press, 1994), p. 5.

9. Lois Marie Gibbs, "Celebrating Ten Years of Triumph," *Everyone's Backyard* 11 (February 1993): 2.

10. Szasz, *Ecopopulism,* pp. 6, 69–72. See also "The Grassroots Movement for Environmental Justice," *Everyone's Backyard* 11 (February 1993): 3.

11. Robert D. Bullard, ed., *Confronting Environmental Racism: Voices from the Grassroots* (Boston: South End Press, 1993), p. 9.

12. Cynthia Hamilton, "Coping with Industrial Exploitation," in Bullard, *Confronting Environmental Racism,* p. 63.

13. Robert D. Bullard, *Dumping in Dixie: Race, Class, and Environmental Quality,* 2d ed. (Boulder, CO: Westview Press, 1994), p. xiii.

14. Stella M. Capek, "The 'Environmental Justice' Frame: A Conceptual Discussion and an Application," *Social Problems* 40 (February 1993): 8.

15. Bunyan Bryant and Paul Mohai, eds., *Race and the Incidence of*

Environmental Hazards: A Time for Discourse (Boulder, CO: Westview Press, 1992), pp. 1–2.

16. The Sierra Club, National Wildlife Federation, Audubon Society, Environmental Defense Fund, Environmental Policy Institute/Friends of the Earth, Greenpeace, etc.

17. See Dana A. Alston, ed., *We Speak for Ourselves: Social Justice, Race and Environment* (Washington, DC: Panos Institute, 1990), p. 3; "From the Front Lines of the Movement for Environmental Justice," *Social Policy* 22 (Spring 1992): 12; Robert D. Bullard, "Anatomy of Environmental Racism and the Environmental Justice Movement," in Bullard, *Confronting Environmental Racism,* pp. 22–23; Pat Bryant, "Toxics and Racial Justice," *Social Policy* 20 (Summer 1989): 51.

18. "Do Environmentalists Care About Poor People?" *U.S. News and World Report,* April 2, 1984, p. 52. See also Matthew Rees, "Black and Green," *New Republic,* March 2, 1992, pp. 15–16.

19. Bryant and Mohai, *Race and the Incidence of Environmental Hazards,* p. 6.

20. Janet Kreger, "Ecology and Black Student Opinion," *Journal of Environmental Education* 4 (Spring 1973): 30–34.

21. Carl Anthony, "Why African Americans Should Be Environmentalists," *Earth Island Journal,* Winter 1990, pp. 43–44.

22. Paul Mohai, "Black Environmentalism," *Social Science Quarterly* 71 (December 1990): 744. See also Frederick H. Buttel and William L. Flinn, "Social Class and Mass Environmental Beliefs: A Reconsideration," *Environment and Behavior* 10 (September 1978): 433–50.

23. Alston, *We Speak for Ourselves,* p. 3.

24. Henry Vance Davis, "The Environmental Voting Record of the Congressional Black Caucus," in Bryant and Mohai, *Race and the Incidence of Environmental Hazards,* pp. 55–63; "Do Environmentalists Care About Poor People?" p. 52; "Beyond White Environmentalism," *Environmental Action,* January/February 1990, pp. 19, 27.

25. Dorceta Taylor, "Can the Environmental Movement Attract and Maintain the Support of Minorities?" in Bryant and Mohai, *Race and the Incidence of Environmental Hazards,* p. 38.

26. Such indicators as money (e.g., donations to environmental causes), politics (e.g., attendance at meetings), legal action (e.g., participating in litigation), education (e.g., attending courses, workshops), nature (e.g., visits to national parks), wildlife (e.g., hunting/fishing),

membership affiliation, and so forth, may not unveil levels of black interest in environmental issues.

27. Dorceta E. Taylor, "Blacks and the Environment: Toward an Explanation of the Concern and Action Gap between Blacks and Whites," *Environment and Behavior* 21 (March 1989): 175–98.

28. Barbara Deutsch Lynch, "The Garden and the Sea: U.S. Latino Environmental Discourse and Mainstream Environmentalism," *Social Problems* 40 (February 1993): 108–18. See also "Beyond White Environmentalism," pp. 24–27.

29. Regina Austin and Michael Schill, "Black, Brown, Poor & Poisoned: Minority Grassroots Environmentalism and the Quest for Eco-Justice," *Journal of Law and Public Policy* 1 (Summer 1991): 79.

30. The CRJ was founded in 1963 after the assassination of black activist Medgar Evers, church bombings in Birmingham, Alabama, and other anti–civil rights activities.

31. See Karl Grossman, "Environmental Racism," *Crisis* 98 (April 1991): 17.

32. See Charles Lee, "Toxic Waste and Race in the United States," in Bryant and Mohai, *Race and the Incidence of Environmental Hazards,* pp. 10–16, 22–27; Rosemari Mealy, "Charles Lee on Environmental Racism," in Alston, *We Speak for Ourselves,* p. 8; Paul Mohai and Bunyan Bryant, "Environmental Racism: Reviewing the Evidence," ibid., pp. 163–69; Grossman, "Environmental Racism," pp. 16–17; Grossman, "From Toxic Racism to Environmental Justice," *E: The Environmental Magazine* 3 (May/June 1992): 30–32; Dick Russell, "Environmental Racism," *Amicus Journal* 11 (Spring 1989): 22–25; Bryant, "Toxics and Racial Justice," pp. 49–50.

33. Bullard, *Confronting Environmental Racism,* p. 3.

34. Ibid.

35. Grossman, "Environmental Racism," p. 31. See also Bullard, *Confronting Environmental Racism,* p. 19.

36. Bullard, *Dumping in Dixie,* p. xv. See also Bullard, *Confronting Environmental Racism,* pp. 10–13, 15–22; Bullard, "Race and Environmental Justice in the United States," *Yale Journal of International Law* 18 (1993b): 319–35.

37. Bullard, *Unequal Protection,* p. xvi.

38. Bullard, "Conclusion: Environmentalism with Justice," in Bullard, *Confronting Environmental Racism,* p. 195.

39. Memorandum, William Clinton, February 11, 1994; "Not in My Backyard," *Human Rights* 20 (Fall 1993): 27–28; Bryant and Mohai, *Race and the Incidence of Environmental Hazards,* p. 5; Grossman, "The People of Color," p. 287.

40. Michel Gelobter, "Toward a Model of 'Environmental Discrimination,' " in Bryant and Mohai, *Race and the Incidence of Environmental Hazards*, pp. 64–73. For a contrary view, see Mohai and Bryant, "Environmental Racism," p. 164.

41. Leonard Gianessi, Henry M. Peskin, and Edward Wolff, "The Distributional Effects of Uniform Air Pollution Policy in the United States," *Quarterly Journal of Economics* 93 (May 1979): 281.

42. Ibid., pp. 281–96.

43. Gelobter, "Model of 'Environmental Discrimination,' " p. 72.

44. Vicki Been, "What's Fairness Got to Do with It? Environmental Justice and the Siting of Locally Undesirable Land Uses," *Cornell Law Review* 78 (September 1993): 1014–15. See also Rachel D. Godsil, "Remedying Environmental Racism," *Michigan Law Review* 90 (November 1991): 394; Rees, "Black and Green," pp. 15–16; Grossman, "Toxic Racism to Environmental Justice," p. 35.

45. "Beyond White Environmentalism," p. 21. See also Russell, "Environmental Racism," pp. 25–30.

46. Alice L. Brown, "Environmental Justice: New Civil Rights Frontier," *Trial* 29 (July 1993): 48, 51–52. See also Bullard, *Dumping in Dixie,* pp. xiii–xiv; " 'Environmental Racism': It Could Be a Messy Fight," *Business Week,* May 20, 1991, p. 116.

47. Brown, "Environmental Justice," p. 52; Been, *"Fairness,"* 1993, pp. 1084–85; Godsil, "Remedying Environmental Racism," pp. 420–26. See also C. Miller, "Efficiency, Equity and Pollution: The Case of Radioactive Waste," *Environment and Planning* 19 (1987): 913–18.

48. Grossman, "Environmental Racism," p. 15.

49. See Martin V. Melosi, *Coping with Abundance: Energy and Environment in Industrial America* (Philadelphia: Temple University Press, 1985), pp. 296–97. See also Samuel Hays, *Beauty, Health, and Permanence: Environmental Politics in the United States,* 1955–1985 (New York: Cambridge University Press, 1987).

50. In the late nineteenth and early twentieth centuries, urban environmentalists formed many local groups to confront the impacts of industrialization and urbanization, although they did not dominate the emerging new environmental movement or give attention to matters of

race and class. See Martin V. Melosi, "Environmental Reform in the Industrial Cities: The Civic Response to Pollution in the Progressive Era," in *Environmental History: Critical Issues in Comparative Perspective,* ed. Kendall E. Bailes (Lanham, MD: University Press of America, 1985), pp. 494–515.

51. Grossman, "Toxic Racism to Environmental Justice," pp. 34–35.

52. See Judith Rees, "Equity and Environmental Policy," *Geography* 76 (October 1991): 292–303; Alston, *We Speak for Ourselves,* pp. 32–33; Bryant, "Toxics and Racial Justice," p. 52.

53. Allan Schnaiberg, "Redistributive Goals versus Distributive Politics: Social Equity Limits in Environmental and Appropriate Technology Movements," *Sociological Inquiry* 53 (Spring 1983): 214. See also John A. Hird, "Environmental Policy and Equity: The Case of Superfund," *Journal of Policy Analysis and Management* 12 (1993): 323–35; Peter Nijkamp, "Equity and Efficiency in Environmental Policy Analysis: Separability versus Inseparability," in *Distributional Conflicts in Environmental-Resource Policy,* ed. Allan Schnaiberg et al. (New York: St. Martin's, 1986), pp. 61–73.

54. Bullard, *Unequal Protection,* p. 19.

55. A. Myron Freeman III, "Distribution of Environmental Quality," in *Environmental Quality Analysis: Theory and Method in the Social Sciences,* ed. Allen V. Kneese and Blair T. Bower (Baltimore: Johns Hopkins University Press, 1972), p. 277.

56. Austin and Schill, "Black, Brown, Poor & Poisoned," 71. For a broad philosophical view of environmental justice, see Peter S. Wenz, *Environmental Justice* (Albany: State University of New York Press, 1988).

4

John R. McNeill

Of Rats and Men

A Synoptic Environmental History
of the Island Pacific

The Pacific and its islands have long held allure for roman-
tics and scientists alike. The ocean's great size and galaxies
of islands make it as appealing to botanists and biogeog-
raphers as to beachcombers. It also has seductive charms
for those interested in environmental history, in the changing mutual influence of human communities and the earth,
air, water, and life forms that sustain them. Recently, two
books have appeared that emphasize the relevance of the
environmental history of Easter Island to that of Planet
Earth.[1] But Easter Island, like most Pacific islands—indeed, most islands anywhere—has had a tumultuous environmental history. Evolution and history have conspired to give
island people especially unstable environments.

The island world of the Pacific shows the transforming

From *Journal of World History* 5, no. 2 (Fall 1994): 299–341. Copy-
right ©1994, University of Hawaii Press. Reprinted by permission.

power of intrusive species, including *Homo sapiens*, in their efforts to secure niches for themselves. For humans, that effort includes economic activity, which is particularly capable of changing environments when organized on large scales; in the case of the Pacific, this has happened primarily through market integration. The power to transform is greatly amplified by the effects of remoteness from the earth's continental hothouses of biological and cultural evolution. Isolation over millions of years caused Pacific ecosystems to become labile, that is, prone to sudden change.

The pattern of environmental history of the Pacific islands exhibits eras of calm interrupted by spurts of torrential change, like the punctuated equilibrium of evolutionary biology, although in this case equilibria often look more punctured than punctuated. The pace of Pacific environmental history has been governed by spurts and lulls in human transport and communication throughout the ocean. The chief determinant of these spurts and lulls has been technology, and for this reason I divide the story, once humankind appears on the stage, into ages of the outrigger, the sailing ship, and the steamship. The direction of change, since humans intruded, has been toward ecological homogenization, within the limits defined by climate, soils, and the susceptibility of ecosystems to change.

The Prehuman Pacific

The Pacific Ocean accounts for one-third of the Earth's surface and half the ocean area. It has about 25,000 islands. I focus on the oceanic islands, not those close to the rim, and still less on the continental rim itself. There is admittedly a certain arbitrariness in this, and distortion, for the history of Micronesia, Melanesia, and Polynesia, especially recently, is linked to the rim. But delimitations are necessary, and with these choices, about 7,500 islands remain.[2]

The great majority of the Pacific islands were born barren of life, basaltic pimples on the sea's surface. New Zealand is the chief exception: it is among the "continental islands" of the western Pacific, together with Fiji, the Solomons, and others to the west. New Zealand already had life forms when it spun off from Gondwanaland 80 million years ago and remained until recently a sanctuary for species of the Cretaceous. Life arrived on other islands by accident or by drift. Some plants arrived by air; seeds carried in the digestive tracts of birds account for 40 percent of Hawaii's early plants.[3] Either the first invaders could float well enough, in air or water, to cross stretches of ocean, or their seeds could survive a voyage in some avian gut. At times of lower sea level (glacial epochs), land bridges linked, or nearly linked, many islands in the far western Pacific, so some species colonized without being notably good floaters or stowaways. In the eastern Pacific only the best travelers arrived and survived. Consequently, the western islands, especially Melanesia, have far greater biodiversity than do the eastern islands of Polynesia. Before European impact, Bougainville in the Solomons had several thousand plant species, while Easter Island had only thirty. Hawaii acquired new species at the modest rate of one every 100,000 years. Newer islands have fewer species, and atolls that became hospitable to terrestrial life only in the past few thousand years (thanks to the fall in sea level in the late Holocene) are impoverished. Vostok in Kiribati had a prehuman flora of only three species.[4] Mammals found it hard to get anywhere in the island Pacific; only bats and rats successfully colonized east of New Guinea. Almost all species derive from Asia, with a tiny proportion from the Americas, so the Pacific had an attenuated Indo-Malayan biota. As a rule of thumb, the farther from Indonesia, the more impoverished the biota and, in consequence, the less resilient to disturbance. This attenuation is strong for land species, less strong for marine species, and nonexistent for oceanic birds.

The isolation of Pacific ecosystems meant opportunities for adaptive radiation: the evolution of new species occupying niches that elsewhere were already filled. Darwin's finches of the Galapagos are the classic example. On islands that had no mammals, reptiles and birds took their places. Thus the Galapagos have giant tortoises, and New Zealand once had giant birds that functioned like browsing or grazing mammals. The paucity of grazing animals meant that plants developed few defenses such as spines, poisonous alkaloids, or bitterness.[5] Remoter islands had high proportions of endemism—that is, of species that existed only there. In the case of Hawaii, as many as 99 percent of species were endemic.[6] All this led to biological vulnerability among terrestrial island species, when obliged to compete for niches with the winners of the more intense continental competitions for survival. This vulnerability increased toward the east and the remoter corners of the Pacific, along a gradient defined by the degree of isolation.

A second source of vulnerability, perhaps more decisive, arose from the late arrival of humankind in the Pacific. Island animals evolved with no experience of the ways of humankind and had acquired no "immunities" to them. Pacific animals were often unwary, easy prey. At the extreme, again the Galapagos, Darwin found birds almost tame, so naively trusting that they would allow him to get within arm's reach. Pacific plants had little experience of fire because natural fires were rare. Thus, few plants were well adapted to fire.

In short, Pacific ecosystems were well adapted to their prehuman circumstances but vulnerable to alien invasion and human impact. The opportunity for speciation and the absence of humankind meant that Pacific island ecosystems diverged over time. Ecological homogenization began with humankind.

The Age of the Outrigger

The biogeographical peculiarities of the island Pacific offered a challenge of the unknown to the first human colonists. Human impact began in New Guinea perhaps 40,000 years ago; elsewhere in Melanesia not until 11,000 to 12,000 years ago. In Micronesia and Polynesia humankind arrived only 3,500 years ago. New Zealand was the last significant Pacific land to acquire human population. Polynesians first landed there within the lifetime of some trees, about 1,000 years ago—although this conventional wisdom is debated.

The Polynesians conspicuously, but other islanders as well, changed their islands in two broad phases. On first arrival, they exploited and depleted the resources easiest to use. This phase might last for centuries. In the second phase, straitened ecological circumstances obliged them to exploit new resources, to utilize new food sources, and to exercise all their ingenuity—or else to emigrate and begin anew in another virgin land.

Island settlers, whether Polynesian, Melanesian, or Micronesian, found no tropical paradises. During the age of island settlement, conditions were worsening because of climatic warming. Between 18,000 and 4,000 years ago, sea level rose about 20 to 30 meters in the southwest Pacific, the most dramatic change in the last 100,000 years. Islands shrank and reefs drowned, diminishing and impoverishing the landscapes.[7]

Many low islands were deficient in fresh water and sustained few useful plants or animals. Higher islands had more fresh water and more varied biotas, and presented fewer constraints. But all islands were subject to environmental disasters: drought, cyclone, tsunami, volcanic eruption, and flood. Initial settlers found their environments unfamiliar on account of high endemism (and, in New Zealand, a cool climate). Reefs and lagoons (absent in New Zealand) were more familiar, as their life forms showed a greater commonality throughout the tropical Pacific. Agriculture presented difficulties because soils were often poor and scant on low islands, fresh water was in short supply, and on all islands seasonality of production was great and food storage problematic.

The islanders invented devices to cope with new environments, such as taro pits to tap the lens of underground fresh water that floats above the salt groundwater on many atolls. In the Marquesas, prone to drought and an unreliable food supply, people raised ensilage technique to a high art. In Fiji, Tahiti, and Hawaii, they developed irrigation systems. Everywhere, settlers needed to exploit more familiar marine resources to compensate for environmental difficulties. In the atolls this meant reef and lagoon life, often abundant, though occasionally vulnerable to environmental shock; in New Zealand it meant mollusks, seals, dolphins, and whales. Even so, hunger was routine, famine frequent, and life usually short.[8]

Faced with these challenges, island settlers sought to transform their new homes into manageable landscapes. They brought notions of suitable landscapes with them and created "transported landscapes" by importing what Crosby, in another context, called a "portmanteau biota."[9] In so doing, they promoted ecological homogenization based on a handful of cosmopolitan species. The Polynesian portmanteau biota consisted chiefly of a few animals (rat, dog, chicken, and pig) and several plants (e.g., coconut, taro, and breadfruit) now widespread throughout the Pacific. Indeed, almost all food crops of the islands are imports.[10] To assist, Polynesians brought fire, humankind's favorite tool for biota management.

The Polynesians significantly changed the fauna of the islands they settled. In Hawaii, half the indigenous bird species (some forty of eighty) were eliminated between the Polynesian arrival (ca. A.D. 400) and that of Captain Cook (1778).[11] New Zealand also lost half its avifauna (some thirty species), including the moa, which weighed up to 200 kilograms and measured almost 2 meters tall. The Marquesas, Cook Islands, and Society Islands had similar extinction rates. Extinctions also followed human settlement in the Chatham Islands, Fiji, and elsewhere. Rats, dogs, and habitat destruction (brought or brought on by human beings) sealed the fate of indigenous birds.

Settlers relied on marine creatures, too, and in some

cases severely depleted their numbers. On Tikopia, mollusks, fish, and turtles suffered sharper declines than birds after the arrival of humankind (about 900 B.C.). After 800 years these declines ended, signaling a transition from the first phase of environmental history to a second. Populations of marine creatures remained somewhat stable from 100 B.C. to A.D. 1800, recovering slightly around 1500, but never approaching densities like those before the first people arrived. Lagoon species, mollusks in particular, declined or vanished with human settlement in tropical Polynesia. Polynesian New Zealanders had hunted fur seals to depletion by 1500 and by the 1760s eradicated them on the North Island. Sea elephants vanished, and sea lions also disappeared from the North Island.

Everywhere people went in the Pacific they hunted and gathered the local fauna. Once initial obstacles of colonization were surmounted, this made for an abundant supply of fish and game—while it lasted. It lasted for generations but not indefinitely, resulting in scarcities and extinctions. This slow crisis required adaptation to a more sophisticated phase of resource use—or emigration.

More significant perhaps than animal extinctions and depletions was the settlers' impact on vegetation. Fire allowed them to replace forest with plant communities more to their liking. Most larger tropical Pacific islands supported rainforest before human settlement. New Zealand was perhaps 85 to 90 percent forest, mostly evergreen podocarp. Settlers torched land to clear the way for shifting cultivation and garden crops. Fire gets out of control easily, especially in drought, and so the areas burned exceeded the needs of agriculture. Anthropic fire vastly extended the fern and shrub savannas. In Fiji, fire cleared wide areas of forest between 3,000 and 1,500 years ago. In New Zealand, Polynesians burned off between one-third to one-half of the postglacial forest area before Cook arrived in 1769.[12] The elimination of browsing birds and the introduction of frequent fire amounted to powerful change in selective pressures on plants—a major part of the ecological revolution created by human occupancy.

In Hawaii, little lowland forest remained when Cook first saw it; Tahiti, Fiji, and most other high islands had been similarly affected. Crops replaced forest trees, but so did weeds that throve on disturbed ground or were compatible with fire. In prehuman Hawaii, most areas burned only once every 700 to 1,000 years, so few native plants (except pili grass) withstood fire well. Human-caused fire opened the field for intruders. Polynesians introduced about thirty-two new plants to Hawaii.[13] Irrigation works extended the domain of cultivation and new plants to dry leeward zones. Wherever they settled, the early Hawaiians, with fire and their portmanteau biota, transformed stable (that is, slowly evolving) ecosystems, the fruit of millions of years of evolution, into a "cultural mosaic" of gardens, swidden fields, tree crops, weeds, and second-growth scrub.[14]

Burning often led to soil degradation. Slopes shorn of protective cover and root mass quickly lose their soil in heavy rains. High rates of erosion, related to forest clearance, affected Fiji in the second to the fourth centuries A.D. Upland cultivation suffered, but swamps created in lowlands helped compensate when converted to taro pits.[15] Hawaii suffered from accelerated erosion, especially from the fourteenth to sixteenth centuries, an era of growing population. In New Zealand, erosion accelerated to three or four times previous rates after human settlement, probably as a consequence of Polynesian burning and deforestation.[16] In many places, sheetwash erosion exposed lateritic soils on which only ferns could flourish. Thus the biological productivity, and the carrying capacity, of many larger islands eventually shrank under the impact of settlement and fire.[17] High and steep islands felt these effects much more than low islands.

Lagoons and reefs felt the human touch even less, although they made a large contribution to sustenance. Fire affected them only through sedimentation increases. Pacific islanders moderated their impact on many ecosystems through restraints on resource use; in many societies, taboos limited the exploitation of reefs, lagoons, and the sea. These taboos often had social or political purposes, but among their effects was reduction in pressures on local ecosystems. Decisions about when and where harvesting might take place were made by men who had encyclopedic knowledge of the local marine biota, "master fishery ecologists."[18] Cultural constraints limited human impact on other elements of island ecosystems, too. Terrestrial hunting, generally of turtles and birds, was subject to magico-religious taboos, or to royal or chiefly privileges. Some societies also protected forests and trees.

Island peoples with limited resource bases had stark incentives to practice conservation. This was especially true on small islands, and it may be no accident that Micronesians observed firm taboos against overuse of reefs and lagoons and maintained turtle and bird sanctuaries. In Darwinian terms, Pacific island environments selected for societies with such cultural characteristics more rigorously than did continental environments. Societies that did not form conservation practices sooner or later suffered for it, as did the Easter Islanders, who appear to have brought themselves to ruin through ecological degradation of their island home.

All the ecological restraints found in Pacific island societies were woven into belief systems and political structures. When and where those systems and structures changed, eroded, or disappeared, so, too, did constraints on environmental overexploitation. This may have happened on Easter Island before Europeans arrived; it certainly happened broadly in the Pacific after their arrival.

Some people maintain that islanders lived in harmony with their environments. Evidence suggests that this is romantic exaggeration. Even the rigorous conservationist incentives of small island ecosystems could not consistently prevail against ordinary human tendencies. Pacific islanders, wherever they were numerous, strongly shaped their environments and frequently degraded them. Conservationist taboos often existed to buttress the power of elite groups, and enforcement could lapse when convenient.[19] Their reverence for nature must not be confused with a conservation ethic. Under the pressure of population growth or the instructions of their rulers, islanders used the tools at hand and inevitably damaged parts of their environments.

On small islands, even ecological angels would have found it hard to keep their numbers in balance with resources. On most islands, people tried to regulate their numbers and moderate population pressures. They were more successful in some times and places—such as the

Society Islands—than others. The practice of seaborne colonization, a perilous business even for the best of navigators, strongly suggests that population sometimes put intolerable strains on limited resources.

Recent research and compelling interpretations of the history of Easter Island support this notion.[20] If anyone had an incentive to limit population growth and depletion of resources, it was Easter Islanders. They first arrived around A.D. 400, but they lost all contact with other people.[21] They were so isolated that they believed theirs was the only land left in the world. Conspicuous forest clearance (visible in pollen diagrams) began about A.D. 800. By 1400 they had cut down almost all the trees at one corner of the island, and by 1600 had cut down almost all trees throughout the island. The island is small enough that whoever cut the last palm surely knew it was the last one. While resources lasted, population mounted, slowly at first, but perhaps doubling every generation after A.D. 1100. It reached a maximum of about 7,000 around 1600, then crashed late in the seventeenth century. In the eighteenth century, apparently after paroxysms of violence and decades of food shortage, inhabitants numbered only 1,000 to 2,000. Other Pacific islanders, who felt no compulsion to cut logs to roll giant statuary from quarries to pedestals, were more cautious about resource depletion and more inclined, like the Tahitians, to resort to infanticide, abortion, and other methods of population control.

Population pressure was the only powerful driving force behind environmental degradation before European impact. Pacific islanders did not engage in much long-distance trade. Interisland trade was often a matter of gift exchange with political motives, and the distances (except around Yap in the Caroline Islands and in the archipelagos just east of New Guinea) and numbers of people involved were small. Pacific islanders developed no powerful new technologies that could radically change their environments; their tool kit consisted of stone implements, domestic animals, and fire. Warfare may have exacerbated burning, but also may have checked population pressure, and, according to Rappaport, it may even have reduced burning.[22] The strong probability is that the extent of human impact on the environment was governed by population and by the inherent potential for disturbance of the islands—greater in the east than the west, and greater in high islands than low ones. Population history probably followed the familiar logistic curve of populations exploiting new but finite ecosystems: slow but accelerating growth from first arrival, which eventually tapers off and approximates equilibrium when carrying capacity is approached.

This pattern apparently describes the New Zealand experience. There, population seems to have grown slowly until about A.D. 1200, after which it burgeoned for three centuries (an era of forest clearance and bird extinction) before slowing down (an era of dietary change and increased violent conflict). Not surprisingly, population history reflects the two phases of environmental history. Human numbers grew quickly in the first phase of comparatively easy resource exploitation, then slowed during the transition to the second phase. On Easter Island, the transition came only at high cost. On Easter Island, Tonga, and perhaps Hawaii, carrying capacity was reached before external shocks rocked the Pacific world. Elsewhere, limits were approached but not exceeded, which had consequences for social hierarchy, political structures, and the likelihood of war, but without the ecological crash that marked Easter Island and that may have been afoot in Hawaii before Captain Cook stepped ashore.[23]

Throughout the centuries of pre-European settlement of the island Pacific, anthropic environmental change took place against a shifting background. On low islands, where coastline change mattered most, tectonic shifts and climate change played a larger role than on high islands. In some cases "natural" environmental change may have overshadowed anthropic change; on an island that stands only a few meters above the sea, subsidence or rise in sea level could make the difference between a habitable island and a wasteland, or no island at all. Even on high islands, such as New Zealand, climate change in the shape of stormier epochs may have led to accelerated erosion. Disentangling "natural" and human causes in environmental change is difficult and often defies consensus among experts.[24]

When Cook entered the Pacific in 1769, he heralded a second surge of change in Pacific environments. In the age of Cook, change was more sudden and thorough than any that had gone before. Human impact in Melanesia had taken place over forty millennia and in Micronesia and Polynesia over anywhere from eight to thirty-five centuries. It had proceeded island by island, rather than enveloping the whole region at once. This pattern changed with Cook. Henceforth, environmental change was chronologically concentrated and geographically dispersed over the entire region.

The Age of Cook, Part I

Sailing Ships and Extraction, 1769–1880

The 1760s were to the Pacific what the 1490s were to Atlantic America. Europeans brought to the Pacific new tools, a new portmanteau biota, and new economic principles and possibilities, all of which combined to disrupt biotic and cultural communities. In Pacific environmental history there is an age of Cook, beginning in 1769 and still in train. I divide it into two parts, the first lasting until about 1880, the second from 1880 to the present.

The two parts parallel the two phases of the environmental history of the pre-European Pacific. The first was characterized by quick exploitation of the most available resources; the second represents adaptation to an impoverished environment that required more work and ingenuity to exploit. The integration of the Pacific into broader flows of goods and people meant that the first phase was much briefer in the age of Cook than in the age of the outrigger, only a century or so long. It also allowed the greater labor requirements of the second phase to be met through migration.

Europeans had sailed the Pacific long before Cook, and so had Japanese, Chinese, Malay, and other mariners. From 1520 to 1760, Spanish, Dutch, French, and British sailors traded and fought around the Pacific Rim. Europeans had sailed perhaps 450 ships across the Pacific by 1769, including two circumnavigators, Byron and Bougainville, but their impact on the oceanic islands, like the impact of Columbus's predecessors in the Americas, came to little. The Spanish Manila galleons (1565–1815), probably the most durable shipping line in world history, account for the vast majority. They passed through Micronesia, but what effect they had on oceanic islands is hard to detect outside of Guam, where they usually paused after 1668. There, Jesuits inaugurated a mission and in converting the population to Christianity gave them influenza and smallpox. Disease, combined with violence by Spanish soldiers, reduced the population by 90 percent. Elsewhere, Europeans had seen perhaps a hundred islands east of New Guinea, but had landed at only about thirty. No mariners dallied outside of Guam except for Alvaro Mendaña and Pedro F. de Quiros in 1595. They stopped for nine weeks at one of the Solomons, and in the Marquesas tried (and failed) to grow maize.[25] There was no great and sudden "Magellanic exchange" across the Pacific, let alone one involving the islands. A few American species became established in the Philippines thanks to the Manila galleons. But in general the ecological isolation of Oceania endured until Cook.[26]

Cook made a difference because he always knew where he was. Earlier European mariners could determine latitude but could only guess how far east or west they might be. Armed with chronometers, Cook and his contemporaries could fix longitude, could describe any location with precision and return to it. European exploration of the Pacific became a less dangerous venture. In this lay peril for the island populations.

The greatest disruption brought on by the arrival of European mariners was human depopulation. Evidence concerning Pacific island populations in the eighteenth and nineteenth centuries is far from ideal, and estimates lately have taken on political shades. Fortunately, there is now an authoritative guide to modern population history in the Pacific from European contact to 1945, the work of the French demographer Jean-Louis Rallu.[27] He uses all imaginable evidence and all the tricks of historical demography, including family reconstitution, and arrives at a grim picture. Depopulation ratios of 10:1 or 12:1 were not rare, and 20:1 was not unknown (the Marquesas). This means that the Pacific's encounter with the Eurasian disease pool was as disastrous as that of the Americas. Declines of 2 or 3 percent a year lasted over decades in many cases, due in part to high sterility (a consequence of sexually transmitted diseases), but more to heightened mortality. In Hawaii between 1834 and 1841, the birthrate was only 19 per 1,000, while the death rate soared to 77 per 1,000.[28] As in the Americas, populations began to stabilize 120 to 150 years after initial contact (roughly 1880–1920 in the Pacific) and then to grow. Most islands have more people today than ever before, but not all; the Marquesas, for example, have only about one-quarter of the population of two centuries ago.[29]

New Zealand represents the other pole from the Marquesas, experiencing a depopulation of about 2.7:1. Estimates of Maori numbers in 1769 vary from a few thousand to 2 million. The most detailed work, that of Ian Pool, suggests something in the range of 100,000—just what Cook guessed.[30] The Maori declined until the 1890s, under the impact of new diseases and dispossession from their lands.

Taking the Pacific as a whole, diseases surely did the most damage. New infections ran amok among island populations with no immunities. While epidemics raged, traditional taboos and hygienic practices were abandoned. Migration to new, growing ports undermined sanitation, promoting gastrointestinal infections, tuberculosis, smallpox, measles, and other contagious diseases.

Simultaneously, the islands lost people through enslavement, "blackbirding" (forced labor recruitment), and labor migration. Many island men joined whaling ships and never came home again. In 1850 some 4,000 Hawaiians were sailing the seven seas, a considerable proportion of the young male population.[31] Peruvian labor recruiters (slavers) took 3,500 Polynesians, mostly Easter Islanders, to work Peru's guano and sugar in 1862 and 1863; by 1866, almost all were dead. About 100,000 men left Melanesia to work the cane fields of Queensland and Fiji between 1860 and 1900; about one-third never returned. Depopulation occasioned by labor exodus in Melanesia reached 0.5 percent each year at its height, accounting for one-quarter or one-fifth of the general decline.[32] Labor migration also promoted circulation of diseases around the Pacific, contributing to higher death rates. Epidemics following the slave raids on Easter Island nearly exterminated the remaining population. Labor migration presumably increased traffic of a variety of other organisms such as food crops, weeds, small animals, and insect pests, and thus contributed to the ecological homogenization of the islands.

The human demographic catastrophe affected other creatures on land and at sea. However variable from island to island, depopulation everywhere destabilized anthropic landscapes and opened niches for other species. At sea, it probably permitted reef and lagoon life a chance to recover where human pressures had depleted it. But on land, the collapse had consequences more complex than a simple return to more "natural" conditions. If agricultural area diminished in proportion to population, then perhaps 90 percent of cultivated land fell out of use. In 1840, cultivation on Tonga appeared "entirely neglected" to an American visitor.[33] Where horticulture had relied on terraces or irrigation, as in Hawaii, labor shortage brought these to ruin, promoting soil erosion. Land abandonment opened the way for forest recovery—a massive fallowing. In Fiji, the bush reclaimed land from villages abandoned around 1860.[34] Second-growth forest must have spread, but on many islands newly arrived grazing animals checked this process. They were part of a Noah's ark of alien species introductions to the Pacific in the age of Cook, some intentional, but many accidental. Their effect was to destabilize island ecosystems, then to further their homogenization.

Grazing animals found good forage on abandoned lands, whereas tall forest would not have suited them so well. The ecological vacuum created by human depopulation helped goats, cattle, and pigs to colonize widely. Their numbers grew exponentially in the absence of predators and initially of diseases as well. In one documented instance, in the Galapagos, three goats released in 1959 became 20,000 goats by 1971.[35] Whalers often stranded goats on Pacific islands so as to ensure a ready food supply, hoping for and often achieving caprine population explosions. Cattle were introduced to Hawaii in 1793, and by 1845 had become a pest, eating and trampling crops. Teeth and hooves were enemies new to Pacific plants, many of which could not survive the attentions of cattle and goats.[36] This spelled opportunity for alien weeds able to coexist with grazing animals. Hawaii acquired at least 111 new plant species between 1769 and 1838, and has almost 5,000 alien species today. Some, like Brazil's guava and Central American clidemia, are pernicious weeds that thrive on the conditions humankind and grazing animals have created. Hawaii now has a pantropical biota, with plants from India, China, Australia, and the Americas, as well as some temperate invaders such as gorse and broom.

Other alien species triggered far-reaching effects. Hawaii acquired mosquitoes for the first time in 1826 and the *Aedes aegypti* in the 1890s, providing vectors for the transmission of new tropical diseases.[37] New rodents, particularly the brown and Norway rats, upset every island's ecology. Breeding into the millions, they flourished to the detriment of birds, the Polynesian rat, crops, and wild plants.[38] Rats' devotion to certain seeds affected the species composition of Hawaiian forests. Rats were the single most consequential alien intruder and ought to be considered the shock troops of ecological imperialism in the Pacific. The bird life of New Zealand and Hawaii, already reduced in variety since the arrival of Polynesians, suffered further depredations from the new rats. Their powerful effect on unprepared bird life is especially clear in the case of Lord Howe Island, which had no human population until the eighteenth century. Once, the island had fifteen or sixteen species of land birds, of which three became extinct between 1788 and 1870 under the impact of European sailors and settlers. There were no further extinctions until 1918, when *Rattus rattus* first arrived and began to feast on birds' eggs. Five further extinctions followed in short order before a second era of stability.

In New Zealand, where the process of exotic invasion is

well documented, intrusive species revolutionized the biotic landscapes after European settlement began in 1840. Many exotics were intentionally introduced, some by "acclimatization societies" formed for that purpose. Their impact sometimes proved beneficial from the settlers' point of view, for food-producing capacity multiplied with the arrival of potatoes, grains, and livestock. But native species suffered from the competition. Deer, rabbits, and opossums have had a notorious effect on native trees and grasses, which have been widely replaced by alien species compatible with these creatures. New Zealanders especially liked game animals, notably deer, which their nonpatrician forebears had not been permitted to hunt in Britain.

Several species were intentionally introduced to control runaway populations of earlier introductions. Frequently the hired assassins ignored their missions and attacked more vulnerable native species. In New Zealand the introduction of cats, stoats, weasels, and ferrets, intended to control rats, led to further decreases among native birds. The mongoose was introduced to Fiji in 1873 to curb rats in cane fields, but instead it extinguished seven native bird species. (The same story was repeated in Jamaica in the late nineteenth century.) Biological pest control in fragile ecosystems is an unpredictable business.

Elsewhere, new crops became established. Between 1821 and 1846, one valley on Oahu (Anahulu) acquired watermelon, corn, tobacco (perhaps not beneficial), cabbage, beans, oranges, limes, lemons, guava, cucumber, squash, red peppers, coffee, and rice. Many of these aliens colonized on their own, replacing native species in gashes left behind by human depopulation.

The arrival of Europeans and their portmanteau biota was a disaster for lowland organisms and soils in the Pacific islands. Many native species suffered extinction, and many more found their domains reduced under the onslaught of the invaders. Initially the highlands felt less impact. All this disturbance, extinction, and replacement involved unconscious ecological teamwork, as one invader cleared the path for the next.

Pacific islands—and Pacific waters—were also vulnerable to ecological change that came through the economic activity of human intruders, European, Euro-American, and Japanese. In 1784 Britain reduced its tea duty from 119 percent to 12 percent, bringing tea from the palace to the cottage and bringing the world to Canton. Except for whaling, all the nineteenth-century pillaging of the Pacific—for sandalwood, sealskins, bêche-de-mer, in some cases even timber—was done for the Chinese market. European, American, and Australian merchantmen organized the exchange, in which Pacific island products were acquired for Western manufactured goods, then exchanged for Chinese silk and tea. From the 1790s to 1850, a world-girdling "triangular trade" linked the Pacific island economies and ecosystems to Europe, North America, and China, with the most powerful consequences for the smallest and least integrated.

While rats feasted on the native bird life of the Pacific, men energetically fell on the marine life. They began with fur seals, which maintained breeding colonies on cooler shores. Before the 1770s, seals had been hunted haphazardly, almost only in New Zealand; after 1770, they aroused the attention of sealers eager to sell skins to China.

Australians and Americans descended on southern New Zealand, especially between 1790 and 1810, working with "reckless efficiency," butchering seals as easily as "men kill hogs in a pen with mallets."[39] Bleaker islands in the sub-Antarctic—the Chathams, Macquarie, Auckland, Campbell—attracted sealing parties, mostly Americans, between 1800 and 1830. Among the best sealing grounds were the Juan Fernandez Islands, which sent 3 million sealskins to China in only seven years after 1782. By 1824, seals became hard to find there and until recently were believed extinct. The sealers put themselves out of business by 1830. In two human generations the fur seals of the Pacific had almost disappeared.

Whalers showed no more restraint. If they learned anything from the short history of Pacific sealing, it was not conservation but urgency: they sought to get their share while the supply lasted. The destruction of Pacific whale populations is one chapter of a long human assault on whales. The pattern is clear: wherever new technology permitted or new whaling grounds were found, men quickly overexploited whale stocks. All whales provided oil from blubber, which was used as a lubricant or as fuel in lamps; baleen whales also provided whalebone, the plastic of the nineteenth century, used in corsets and umbrellas among other things. Sperm whales provided the most valuable oil, and those that had ulcers also provided ambergris, worth several hundred dollars per ounce in China as a spice and aphrodisiac.

Pacific whaling opened up in the late 1780s. East India Company monopoly rights kept Britons and Australians from exploiting whales until 1801, giving the French and

Americans a head start. By 1820, New Englanders dominated the business, concentrating on the nutrient-rich Humboldt Current off Chile and Peru. Whalers first devoted themselves to right whales, found chiefly in temperate latitudes. These were easiest to catch because they swim slowly, prefer inshore waters, and float when killed. New Zealand right whales, first hunted heavily around 1830, were depleted by 1850; they remain rare today. Sperm whales, found in deep seas, usually within 30 degrees of the equator, held greater commercial value. By the 1840s sperm whales attracted 500 to 700 ships and 15,000 to 20,000 men to the Pacific each year, mostly American. The other target was the humpback, which crossed the tropics on annual migrations. Tropical whaling flourished between 1835 and 1860. The northern Pacific was worked from Honolulu, which first developed as a whaling port. Southern whaling ports were Hobart, Tasmania and Russell, New Zealand. Japanese and Russians hunted whales in the northwest Pacific, generally only in coastal waters until 1920. Whalers reduced numbers so much that whaling virtually ceased until technological innovations around the turn of the century made it possible to hunt rorquals (larger whales).[40] Whaling also affected island vegetation, since reducing blubber to oil required fuelwood. Hawaii once produced half a million barrels of whale oil a year.[41]

The marine creatures of island lagoons also attracted commercial attention in the nineteenth century. Sea slugs or sea cucumbers (known to connoisseurs as bêche-de-mer) enjoyed a strong market in China, where through the efforts of Yankee traders they found their way into countless soups—they are alleged to have aphrodisiac qualities. Fiji produced sea slugs in quantity, especially between 1828 and 1850. It is hard to assess the impact on lagoon ecology, but the sole authority believes it depleted Fijian lagoons.[42] Truk produced half a million tons of sea slugs annually around 1900. The trade also affected vegetation. Drying sea slugs required keeping fires burning day and night, consuming "enormous amounts of timber" in Fiji; Ward calculates that it required 1 million cubic feet of fuel and devastated coastal vegetation.[43] Even palm groves were cut to supply drying houses. Whatever the impact, it did not last; the trade withered away.

Sandalwood, an aromatic tree that can reach 20 meters in height, was common throughout the high islands of the tropical Pacific (and in South and Southeast Asia). Pacific islanders had used it. But the Chinese market, long fed from India, focused on Pacific sources in the nineteenth century. Sandalwood went into ornamental woodwork, and its fragrant oil was used in incense, perfumes, and medicines. Traders aware of its worth in Canton went first to Fiji (1804–16), then the Marquesas (1815–20). Next they turned to Hawaii (1811–31), where a royal monopoly expedited depletion, and lastly to Melanesia, especially the New Hebrides (1841–65). In Hawaii, kings and chiefs put thousands of commoners to work cutting sandalwood. They burned dry forests to make the precious timber easy to find by its scent (only its heartwood was valuable, so charred trunks were fine). In the heyday of the Hawaiian trade, between 1 and 2 million kilograms went to China every year. Eventually only the poorest and remotest specimens remained. Hawaiian royalty even tried to exploit stands in the New Hebrides by outfitting two ships for Vanuatu in 1829 (they were never heard from again). Sandalwood disappeared quickly and in most places scarcely returned. The commercial exploitation of 150 years ago made an enduring impact on the species composition of Pacific vegetation.[44]

Other trees became the target of timber merchants, especially in Hawaii. In the late nineteenth century, road construction, the presence of draft animals, and the availability of metal tools gave rise to a logging industry. It focused on koa, a native acacia that makes fine cabinet and furniture wood. Some Hawaiian koa went for railroad ties in the United States.[45]

New Zealand forests also felt the impact of nineteenth-century commerce. Northern New Zealand once had magnificent stands of kauri, a hardwood admired by shipbuilders. These disappeared between 1790 and 1860, primarily to satisfy the timber requirements of Britain's Royal Navy. The only Polynesian islands where Europeans settled on a large scale in the nineteenth century, New Zealand had its vegetation and soils dramatically affected by nineteenth-century economic forces. By 1900 stockmen and farmers had burned off perhaps half the forests in existence at the time of European settlement. In the 1890s alone, 36,000 square kilometers of forest, equal to 14 percent of New Zealand's land area, disappeared. This spoliation continued uninterrupted into the twentieth century.

Smaller trades in the nineteenth century had ecological impacts. The pig and pork trade from Tahiti to Sydney (1793–1825) experienced a boom, with consequences for Tahitian vegetation. The tortoiseshell (actually hawksbill turtle) trade led to a sharp depletion of the turtle population. Pearls, pearl shell, coral moss, and birds' nests were traded to China from the Society Islands and elsewhere.

Mother-of-pearl oyster, especially sought for buttons, found a strong market after 1802, with 150,000 metric tons extracted from the Society Islands. Here and in the Cook Islands, the only sizable oyster banks in the Pacific, supplies shrank after 1820, and the trade shriveled accordingly. Today, natural stocks remain close to zero.

Throughout the nineteenth century, commerce had powerful effects on the Pacific islands. This was true politically because disruption followed the development of new forms and sources of wealth and new technologies of destruction (guns). It was true economically, as many islanders for the first time found themselves linked to long-distance trade networks they generally knew little about and therefore could not often use to their advantage. It was also true ecologically for two major reasons, two sides of the same coin.

First, the ecological isolation of the islands at the beginning of the age of Cook made them vulnerable to rapid disruption. Pacific island birds were not equipped to compete for niche space with rats, cats, and mongooses. Pacific islanders' immune systems could not recognize tuberculosis and smallpox. Pacific plants had not adapted to an environment of fire. This accounts for the spectacular impact of exotic introductions.

The second reason is the cultural effect of isolation. The cultural configurations of island societies often contributed to vulnerability to ecological and other disruptions. Where firm hierarchy prevailed, as in Fiji and Hawaii, the extractive trades of the nineteenth century recommended themselves to chiefs and kings, who saw profit in them. They organized the labor, sold the products to traders, and participated in the ecological depletion of their islands. Some no doubt felt they needed to do so to acquire the guns needed for defense and available only from Europeans and Americans. Traders operated in the Pacific at great financial and personal risk; they wanted to make money fast and had no stake in preserving any resource. Politics and ecology interacted in unfortunate ways when confronted with new commercial opportunities, a story with many parallels around the world.

The constraints island societies had devised against resource depletion often disintegrated with the cultural transformations of the nineteenth century. Christianity lacks taboos on resource use, though it has strong taboos on abortion and infanticide. It is a continental ideology, not an island one. Mission education and its public successors neglected local ecological knowledge, so that in the nineteenth and twentieth centuries, successive generations understood less and less of the cycles of nature. The price mechanism and the doctrine of individual advancement contributed to the corrosion of traditional restraints on overexploitation. The forests, pasture, lagoons, and reefs of the Pacific suffered the fate of the seal rookeries and whaling grounds. These often well-regulated common resources turned into unregulated commons, producing unhappy effects noted by observers from Aristotle to Garrett Hardin.[46]

The rapid and widespread environmental change in the early age of Cook had two driving forces, one ecological, the other economic. The ecological force was the sudden uniting of Pacific ecosystems with those of the wider world, combined with inherent lability. The economic force was concentrated demand, as huge markets became connected suddenly to small zones of supply in the Pacific. The demand for whale oil, for sandalwood, even for sea slugs focused the consumer demand of millions in America, Europe, and China on Fiji, Hawaii, Tahiti, and the whaling grounds. Next to these impacts, the environmental change attributable to natural causes, such as climate change, seems paltry.

One can see an era of accelerated change from about 1790 to 1850, followed by a slackening in the rate of change from 1850 to 1880. The important exotic species (mammals and microorganisms) had arrived early in the century, and their greatest impact came at an early stage when their populations mushroomed. The rate of human depopulation slowed and in most islands stopped before the end of the century. The slackening in rates of change is impossible to demonstrate satisfactorily, given the complexities of population biology among dozens of introduced and native species. Much clearer is the slackening derived from the decline of the China market. Whale oil aside, the major products exported from the Pacific after 1780 went to China. By 1850, Chinese tea could be had for opium, without hunting down the last seals or sandalwood. As the British East India Company converted tracts of Bengal to opium production, China's commercial horizons shifted, and the Pacific trade lapsed into insignificance. Also, the Taiping Rebellion (1850–64) convulsed China, reducing its appetite for Pacific specialty goods. After decades of hunting or gathering, seals, sandalwood, and sea slugs grew scarce; the China trade had skimmed off the cream of exploitable resources. Until commercial production replaced commercial hunting and gathering, the ecological impact of the age of Cook abated.[47]

The Age of Cook, Part II

Steamships and Plantations, 1880 to the Present

As plantation agriculture expanded, so did regular networks of transportation and communication, organized within the context of colonial economies. In consequence, environmental change accelerated once again. The formal end of colonialism in the mid- and late twentieth century did not make much difference, in environmental matters at least. Environmental change in the Pacific since 1880 has been comparatively well documented. I offer only the barest outlines of the story and a brief assessment of why things took the direction they did.

Toward the end of the nineteenth century, European and American interest in the Pacific heightened, as it had in the 1760s, primarily for geopolitical reasons. Ambitious great powers desired a presence in the Pacific, preferably colonies and coaling stations. Keeping these supplied required regular shipping, which was established for the first time. Steamships shortened traveling time, allowing organisms a better chance of surviving the trip from one place to another in the wide Pacific. The Panama Canal, completed in 1914, sharply lowered the costs of sailing between the Pacific islands and the economic powers of the day. The links grew tighter still during World War II, when the movement of men and goods around the Pacific accelerated still further. Air travel during the war and civilian air travel after 1950 reduced formidable distances to trifles and permitted the introduction of new alien organisms that did not otherwise travel well. As before, advances in human transport caused considerable ecological change, almost all of it unintended and unforeseen.[48]

Most of the consequential exotic intrusions into the Pacific had taken place before the 1880s. It took time for invasive species to make their way everywhere they could, so their colonizations continued to ripple throughout the Pacific. In the Cook Islands, cats, introduced in the nineteenth century, exterminated indigenous birds throughout the twentieth century. New Zealand also continued to lose native birds. Nibblers and browsers, such as rabbit and deer, had degraded New Zealand forests and pastures by 1930–50. The most remote islands did not feel the impact of exotic species until the twentieth century.[49] At the same time, countless new species invaded. Hawaii, which acquired a new species every 100,000 years in prehuman times, now acquires twenty invertebrates alone every year, mostly by airplane.[50] Here I confine myself to the stories of the tree snake of Guam and the giant African snail.

In the 1970s, people began to notice that the native birds of Guam were disappearing. No one knew why. Eventually the culprit was identified: an introduced snake, *Boiga irregularis*. It climbs trees and devours chicks and fledglings. Guam's avifauna had no experience of such a predator and lacked any defense. Bats and lizards, too, almost disappeared, while the snake's population densities in some places reached 100 per hectare.[51] It provides a classic case of population explosion of an introduced predator. The snake is native to Melanesia; when salvaged war equipment from Melanesia was routed through Guam after 1944, it probably carried snakes, which disembarked. By 1970 the snake had colonized most of the island and was obliterating its food supply. It is likely to spread to other islands, with much the same consequences.[52]

The giant snail *(Achatina fulica)* is native to the East African coast. It was deliberately introduced to Mauritius and Reunion early in the nineteenth century so that French planters could enjoy escargots. But the snail is a superb stowaway, attaching itself to materials of almost any sort. It is hermaphroditic and reproduces prolifically. It entered the South Pacific via Indonesia and the Philippines by 1930. Before World War II, it was established in Papua New Guinea, Micronesia, and Hawaii. It reached Guam during the war. It is now distributed throughout the tropical Pacific, where it is a major crop pest. It has also acquired a beachhead in Florida, where an eight-year-old boy brought some home from Hawaii in 1966. The African snail has also brought indigenous snails to the brink of extinction. It has eliminated a native snail *(Pastula)* from Moorea; that genus now survives only in a reptile tank on the English Channel island of Jersey. In driving out *Pastula* the African snail was helped by an American variety, *Euglandina rosea,* a predator introduced to check the African snail. The American ignored the formidable African and feasted instead on native snails, hastening their demise. Twenty native Hawaiian snails have gone extinct this way. This is an example of attempted biological control of pests gone awry—a common story in twentieth-century Pacific history. About 100 extinctions are attributed to intentionally introduced species that behaved in unexpected ways. Numerous other pests infiltrated the Pacific after 1880, including rabbits, insects, and diseases. Many of them spread during the golden age of Pacific shipping from 1914 to

1965, when two to three vessels sailed weekly along the main shipping routes.[53]

One factor that helped crop pests spread throughout the Pacific was the creation of plantation agriculture, with its monocultural production patterns and emphasis on exports. This improved the prospects of travel and sustenance for the rhinoceros beetle, the coconut beetle, and others that delight in coconut groves, sugarcane fields, and the like.

Plantation agriculture appeared in the middle of the nineteenth century and grew rapidly toward its end. Steamships, colonialism, and, in places such as Fiji, imported indentured labor helped. Pacific plantations reflected, and continue to reflect, the demand for copra, sugar, pineapple, margarine, coffee, and other tropical products.

Plantations invariably bring large-scale environmental change. Broad expanses must be cleared for crops, and generally forest land is preferred, certainly for sugar. On Pacific islands, suitable lowland forest had often already been cleared, so plantations made do with swidden fields. The fuel requirements of sugar boiling contributed to forest clearance in Fiji and Hawaii, as they had in Brazil and the Caribbean. In Hawaii, sugar became a major crop in the 1890s, and by the 1970s occupied 100,000 hectares. Pineapple, introduced early in the nineteenth century, covered up to 30,000 hectares at its peak in the 1950s. Bananas and coffee accounted for smaller areas. Land clearing for commercial crops has been the main cause of plant extinctions in twentieth-century Hawaii, where about 10 percent of the native flora is gone and another 50 percent endangered.

Smaller-scale plantation agriculture appeared in the Society Islands after 1860, at first emphasizing cotton in response to shortages arising from the American Civil War. In the 1920s the Japanese converted Saipan, Tinian, and Rota (acquired from Germany as a League of Nations mandate) into "one vast cane plantation."[54] Most small islands, insofar as they developed plantation agriculture, produced only copra, which in the days of regular interisland shipping found ready markets.

Ranching, which can be considered plantation pastoralism, also contributed to vegetation change. Cattle suppress forest regrowth and favor the success of introduced grasses. Repeated burning has the same effect. Ranching and plantation agriculture intensified the fire regime of much of Hawaii, promoting fire-resistant (mostly African) grasses.[55] There, commercial ranching dates from the middle of the nineteenth century but expanded quickly in the twentieth century. By 1960, half the area of the state was devoted to beef cattle; the proportion declined to a quarter by 1990. As in the "hamburger connection" of Central America since 1960, a large chunk of forest conversion in Hawaii is a result of the beef export trade. Sheep accounted for a fraction of the conversion to pasture. Their numbers varied between 20,000 and 40,000 from 1870 to 1940. Even remote Easter Island felt the ungentle touch of commercial ranching. Sheep first arrived in 1864, when the human population verged on extinction. Commercial sheep ranching began in 1870, and cattle ranching followed. Sheep raising was the mainstay of the Easter Island economy for over a century, until the 1980s, and cattle are still raised there. Ruminants, owned by Chileans, have selected the modern vegetation of Easter Island.

Nowhere has ranching assumed a greater role in environmental change than in New Zealand, which turned into a pastoral plantation. In 1830, forests covered 18 million hectares; in 1980, they had receded to 6 million. In 1840, New Zealand had 8 million hectares of grasslands; in 1980, it had 14 million, two-thirds covered by imported grasses.[56] This was a transformation of the New Zealand landscape in the name of livestock. Stockmen burned off the forests and seeded grasses to run sheep or cattle.[57] From 1840 to 1880, wool led the way. Britain's industrial revolution in textiles promoted the ecological transformation of the South Island's high country. After 1882, when refrigerated ships began to sail from New Zealand to Europe, the focus of forest clearance, settlement, and ecological change shifted to the North Island, which developed an intensive dairy industry. The resulting economy, entirely dependent on the British market for butter, cheese, wool, and meat, provided a fine living for New Zealand. In 1940 it was the richest country in the world in per capita terms. This bounty was achieved with great effort and at the cost of exposing New Zealand soils to erosion, which has ravaged many parts of the country since 1860. Since 1950, pastoral and agricultural productivity has been maintained only through heavy applications of chemical fertilizer, much of which derives from phosphate deposits on other Pacific islands.[58] New Zealand did not make the most of its environmental transformations (millions of cubic meters of good timber have gone up in smoke), but it has not done badly. Other Pacific societies were less fortunate, partly because they had less control over the process.

Forest clearance in the twentieth century has affected all the high islands in the Pacific. In some instances plantation agriculture played the dominant role, while in others subsistence agriculture, driven by population expansion, has done so. In the Solomons, and elsewhere in Melanesia, the richest forests in the tropical Pacific have attracted the timber trade, lately for the Japanese market. Since 1970, timber harvesting has combined with agricultural expansion to reduce forest cover in the Solomons, Fiji, Samoa, and elsewhere in the Pacific, bringing erosion problems, habitat loss, and extinctions.

Extractive activities have changed the Pacific islands. Mining has altered the face of the land. In New Zealand, alluvial gold mining has chewed up the bed of the Clutha River; in New Caledonia and the Solomons, mining has fundamentally changed many localities in recent decades. The biggest copper mine in the world, the Panguna mine, is found on Bougainville. Its slurry has killed all life in the Jaba River and altered the riverbed and delta. In the 1970s, 155,000 metric tons of earth were displaced daily, 99 percent dumped as waste rock or tailings. Phosphate from Makatea in French Polynesia enriched Japanese, New Zealand, and American soils, but mining it destroyed much of the island's surface between 1910 and 1960. Japanese phosphate mining did the same in Palau after 1914.

Nowhere has mining affected the environment as dramatically as on Nauru and Banaba (Ocean Island). On these atolls, seabirds have left deep guano deposits over the millennia, the richest in the world and almost pure phosphate. In 1900 and for a long time before, the phosphate was covered by topsoil and forest. Mining began in 1905 and will end within a decade. About 100 million tons have been extracted, of which two-thirds went to Australia, one-quarter to New Zealand, and the balance to Britain, Malaysia, and Japan. The people of Banaba have not done well, having had their island mined out by 1979. Many Banabans now work for wages on Nauru. Nauruans, of whom there are about 5,000, are more fortunate: none of them needs to work. TheNauruans renegotiated the phosphate mining lease after independence from Great Britain in 1968 and have since become both the least populated state in the world and the richest, with a per capita income greater than that of Saudi Arabia or Switzerland. Nauruans have invested their proceeds, and so they will be rentiers when the phosphate runs out, as they expect it will before the turn of the century. There is little surface left of their island suitable for agriculture: on four-fifths of Nauru, miners have extracted the guano to a depth of 6 or 7 meters, leaving empty pits amid limestone pillars showing where the land surface once was. Recovery of native vegetation may take millennia.[59] This economically logical ecological barbarity is one of the results of the livestock economy in Australia and New Zealand.[60]

Pacific whaling in the twentieth century, as in the nineteenth, qualifies as an extractive industry because no effort to sustain stocks has been effective. The moribund industry revived around the turn of the century, thanks to a Norwegian whaler, Sven Foyn, whose explosive harpoon gun revolutionized whaling. Nineteenth-century Yankee whalers had hunted much like mammoth hunters of the Pleistocene, by throwing a spear into their prey. With the harpoon gun and other inventions, whaling entered the industrial age. Big, fast, deep-diving rorquals became accessible targets; indeed, no whale species were left unhunted. Norwegians dominated whaling from 1900 to 1930 and pioneered the exploitation of the previously undisturbed Antarctic stocks in 1904. By 1914 they had invented the factory ship, which allowed them to process at sea and avoid regulations imposed by the countries (usually Britain) that controlled the islands that previously served as shore bases.

Others soon copied the Norwegian artillery and factory ship, especially Russians and Japanese, who dominated Pacific whaling after 1945. By the late 1930s, blue whales, largest and most valuable of the rorquals, had grown scarce. Fin whales became depleted by 1960, sei whales by 1975. Further technological refinements, such as the use of sonar and satellite imagery, have made whaling scientific, bringing all but Minke whales, smallest of the rorquals, to the edge of extinction all over the world, including the Pacific. The oft-ignored restrictions imposed by the International Whaling Commission (founded in 1946–47) are the only barrier between modern whalers and the final extinction of their prey.

The driving forces behind environmental changes in the Pacific after 1880 are the same as in the first half of the age of Cook—with one alteration and one addition. In both periods, concentrated demand from numerous and distant consumers was focused on small Pacific islands. This gave rise to the plantation agriculture of Fiji and Hawaii, the livestock runs and ranches of New Zealand and Hawaii, and the phosphate mining of Nauru. The ebb and flow of demand for various products in the United States, Japan, Australia, and elsewhere around the Rim has had strong consequences for Pacific island environments. China has disappeared from the position of dominance it held in the nineteenth century, although it may yet return to that position in the twenty-first.

In both periods, advances in transport technology and reductions in transport times and costs brought Pacific ecosystems into ever closer contact with the rest of the world. Most of the important consequences of this trend emerged in the nineteenth century, but many continued into the twentieth. New, exotic species arrived, and those previously introduced were more widely dispersed. Native species continued to suffer the effects of new competitors.

In the twentieth century, as in the nineteenth, population has crucially affected environmental change. The mechanism, however, has fundamentally altered: in the nineteenth century environmental effects resulted from population decline, but in the twentieth century derived from population growth, which from natural increase and immigration filled most islands to historic maxima. By mid-century, Oceania's populations were rising by 3 percent each year; at the end of the century, growth stands at 2.5 percent in Melanesia, a bit less in Micronesia and Polynesia. Population growth required an extension of cultivation, with unhappy consequences for native vegetation and soils. It has often led to intensified use of reefs and lagoons as well.[61]

In addition, temporary population surges resulting from tourism or military presence have affected environments on a few islands. Tahiti, Saipan, and Oahu have experienced both. Tourism has flourished since the 1970s, bringing millions to Pacific islands. Entrepreneurs and developers have radically redesigned coastal districts to suit the preferences of the tourists. Their projects have led to chain reactions of effects on coastal vegetation and soils, reefs and lagoons. Waste disposal on scales never before necessary now vexes several islands. Some tourists are drawn to the Pacific by the ecological distinctions of the islands and serve as a force for nature conservation. The tourist boom is still increasing, and its full effects remain to be seen.

Less predictable temporary surges in population have come with warfare. World War II brought sudden influxes that doubled or tripled island populations, straining local resources. Troops came and went swiftly, as whalers had done a century before. Sometimes they took local men with them, as the Japanese did in Micronesia when they recruited labor battalions for their Southeast Asian campaigns. The isolation of Japanese-held islands late in the war, when the Americans controlled air and sea, led to acute overpopulation and undersupply: all edibles were gathered or hunted by hungry locals and Japanese. At the war's end, islands with Japanese settlement, primarily in the Marianas, were suddenly deflated as their Japanese populations—as much as 90 percent of the total—departed. In the war years, numerous islands, even remote ones that had felt little impact from trade or plantations, experienced the scouring ecological effects of population instability in a concentrated, if brief, form.

Indigenous island populations fluctuated in the twentieth century in response to inducements and discouragements to migration. Recently, islanders everywhere have been migrating to the Pacific Rim and to cities. Samoans have moved in large numbers to New Zealand and the United States. Cook Islanders have left for New Zealand, where they now outnumber those still at home by two to one. Auckland has the world's largest concentration of Polynesians. The decline of shipping and the rise of long-haul air traffic have economically isolated most islands, a bitter irony for those that had abandoned self-sufficiency for participation in the global economy. They can no longer export copra; they must export people.

Such population movements amount to another widespread fallowing, a reduction of pressures on lands and lagoons, as yet less profound than that of the first age of Cook. Once again, this does not necessarily translate into a resurgence of native vegetation and marine life because exotic species are now entrenched, and many are nimble colonizers. On steep land, emigration has meant labor shortage, abandonment, and accelerated erosion as terraces and irrigation channels suffer neglect. Migration to the cities has promoted a new kind of environment, with new problems, the most serious of which is waste disposal. The population mobility of the twentieth century has caused environmental pressures distinct from those of growth or decline.

The additional driving force in Pacific environmental change, almost absent in the first age of Cook but conspicuous in the second, is the colonial and military presence. European colonialism after 1880 favored the development of plantations, mines, and timber concessions. British power over Nauru allowed Australia and New Zealand to obtain phosphate cheaply (royalties to Nauruans were originally £50 per year and remained trivial until 1968). U.S. dominion in Hawaii eased the way for sugar, pineapple, and cattle barons. Japanese control of the Marianas permitted state-supported sugar plantations. But a great deal of the economic and environmental change that took place in the twentieth century resulted not merely from colonialism but chiefly from the linkage to the global economy.

The military impact of the great powers is another matter.

Military occupations led to the forced depopulation of some islands (something the Spanish had done in the Marianas in the seventeenth century). Japanese occupation, though brief, brought some islands of Micronesia and Melanesia into more regular contact with the wider world. World War II helped materially in the dispersal of weeds, insects, and other pests. New Zealand acquired four major crop pests during the war.[62] Lengthy combat, as on Guadalcanal or Okinawa, blistered some islands, with consequences still visible half a century later. Naval bombardment nearly obliterated vegetation on many atolls. The effects of combat, however intense, are not likely to last. On Saipan, the scene of bitter fighting in 1944, vegetation has erased almost all the scars of war, as well as the prewar cane fields. Probably most consequential, and certainly most durable, is the environmental impact of the nuclear programs of the Americans, British, and French.

Nuclear testing began in the Pacific in 1946 when the United States detonated a bomb at Bikini Atoll in the Marshall Islands. The first hydrogen bomb test, also American and oddly titled Operation Greenhouse, was conducted in 1952 on neighboring Eniwetok. It apparently killed off the rat population of the atoll. Britain's nuclear testing began in Australia in 1952, but British hydrogen bomb testing took place in the Gilbert Islands starting in 1957. The French moved their nuclear weapons testing to the Pacific after 1962, when Algerian independence deprived them of their Saharan testing grounds. They took the precaution of incorporating the new sites, the atolls of Moruroa and Fangataufa, into France in 1964, so that any decolonization in French Polynesia would not jeopardize French nuclear testing in the Pacific. All in all, about 250 nuclear tests have taken place in the Pacific since 1945.

The full environmental effects of these tests are difficult to assess because the details are kept secret. The British and French have been more careful in this matter than the Americans. The Bikini Islanders, for example, have attracted considerable study. Evacuated before the first atomic tests, many of them returned to their island early in the 1970s after it was officially declared safe. They were removed once more after this assessment was called into question in the late 1970s. Their health has become a controversial issue. It seems clear that (1) they have unusually high rates of thyroid malignant tumors, miscarriages, and stillbirths; (2) they tend to ascribe all ailments to radiation poisoning; and (3) they have become adept at the politics of nuclear compensation. Since testing ended in 1958, recolonizing plants have covered most of Bikini, although the species composition is quite different from that in 1946. Some plants have attained spectacularly large size. Whether this is an early stage in ecological succession or betokens the triumph of species tolerant of higher levels of radiation is unclear.

The broader consequences of nuclear tests may be great or small. Secrecy makes it difficult to know, one way or another. Atmospheric testing, abandoned last by France in 1974, dispersed fallout throughout the global atmosphere. Undersea testing, abandoned in the 1960s, dispersed radiation through ocean currents. Underground testing, performed only by the French in the Pacific, persisted until a moratorium in 1992. The reefs of Muroroa are impregnated with highly lethal plutonium, some of which is leaking into the sea. The consequences will be durable, since plutonium has a half-life of 24,000 years.

Conclusion

The environmental history of the Pacific exemplifies the costs of splendid isolation—or, more accurately, of the end of isolation. Island ecosystems were highly labile, increasingly so from west to east along the gradient of increasing isolation. Indeed, one might claim the same for their cultural systems. This conferred extraordinary power upon external agents of all biological ranks. Similar patterns of isolation and its breakdown have produced cataclysmic change around the world, in polar latitudes, in rainforest refugia, and on many islands outside the Pacific. In every instance, advances in transport, the process of economic integration, and to some extent the political links of colonial empires and war efforts broke down the barriers of isolation, provoking sudden changes, most of them unfortunate for indigenous organisms and societies. Once the human presence was firmly established, ecosystems, individual immune systems, and sociopolitical systems all proved vulnerable to outside disturbance. It could hardly have been otherwise.

From the biological viewpoint, Pacific environmental history seems to carry a strong overtone of determinism, derived straightforwardly from the penalties of isolation. But from the historical viewpoint, it also bears the mark of accident. Little of the environmental change was desired or intended. No one wanted any but a few of the extinctions. No one wanted the depletions and range contractions of various plants and animals, terrestrial and marine. No one wanted the depopulation of the early age of Cook. Most of these things were unforeseen and unintended consequences of human action. The law of unforeseen consequences is a potent one, in history as in ecology. Only a few environmental changes, such as sandalwood depletion or atomic radiation, could have been expected. They happened because some people—often not Pacific islanders—regarded them as an acceptable or a negligible price to pay for some economic or political gain. The laws, or at least the probabilities, of unequal power are potent as well.

Notes

1. Paul Bahn and John Flenley, *Easter Island, Earth Island* (London: Thames and Hudson, 1992); Clive Ponting, *A Green History of the World* (London: Sinclair-Stevenson, 1991). *The Economist* has printed a story on intrusive species in Hawaii. See *The Economist,* April 10, 1993, pp. 91–92.
2. My approach here to environmental history is more ecological than chemical or physical. Most of the big changes (exceptions such as nuclear radiation and soil erosion are discussed) have been in biological communities, rather than in pollution or the shape of the earth. See J.E. Brodie and R.J. Morrison, "The Management and Disposal of Hazardous Wastes in the Pacific Islands," *Ambio* 13 (1984): 331–33, on the problem represented by pollution. Further, I have little to say here about pelagic fishing. It seems impossible to ascertain the impact of fishing until ca. 1970, when clear signs of overfishing appeared.
3. Sherwin Carlquist, *Hawaii: A Natural History* (Kaua'i: Pacific Tropical Botanical Garden, 1980), pp. 4–5.
4. Patrick D. Nunn, "Recent Environmental Changes on Pacific Islands." *Geographical Journal* 156 (1990): 125–40, 128.
5. F.R. Fosberg, "Vegetation of the Society Islands." *Pacific Science* 46 (1992): 232–50, 237.
6. P.V. Kirch, *The Evolution of the Polynesian Chiefdoms* (Cambridge, UK: Cambridge University Press, 1984), p. 23.

7. N.J. Enright and C. Godsen, "Unstable Archipelagos—Southwest Pacific Environment and Prehistory Since 30,000 B.P.," in *The Naive Lands: Prehistory and Environmental Change in Australia and the Southwest Pacific,* ed. John Dodson (Melbourne: Longman Cheshire, 1992), pp. 160–98, 173–79.

8. There are four major series of skeletons for prehistoric Polynesia (two from Hawaii, one from Tonga, one from the Marquesas). They show that almost no one lived to age fifty, that death rates increased sharply for those over age thirty-five, and that infant and child mortality was highly variable. Kirch, *Polynesian Chiefdoms,* pp. 114–17.

9. Alfred W. Crosby, *Ecological Imperialism: The Biological Expansion of Europe, 900–1900* (Cambridge, UK: Cambridge University Press, 1986), pp. 89–90. See also Alfred W. Crosby, *Germs, Seeds and Animals: Studies in Ecological History* (Armonk, NY: M.E. Sharpe, 1994).

10. Of food crops, only the sweet potato, which came from South America, was not an Asian plant. How it arrived on Pacific islands is subject to controversy. The chicken went everywhere with the Polynesians. Neither dog nor pig made it to Easter Island; pigs were also absent from Polynesian New Zealand. See D.L. Oliver, *Native Cultures of the Pacific Islands* (Honolulu: University of Hawaii Press, 1989), pp. 39–46. Polynesians accidentally introduced a few more animals to Hawaii, such as geckos, skinks, and snails. See Linda Cuddihy and Charles Stone, *Alteration of Native Hawaiian Vegetation: Effects of Humans, Their Activities and Introductions* (Honolulu: University of Hawaii Cooperative National Park Resources Study Unit, 1990), p. 32.

11. S.L. Olson and H.F. James, *Prodromus of the Fossil Avifauna of the Hawaiian Islands* (Washington, DC: Smithsonian Institution, 1982); S.L. Olson and H.F. James, "The Role of Polynesians in the Extinction of the Avifauna of the Hawaiian Islands," in *Quaternary Extinctions: A Prehistoric Revolution,* ed. P.S. Martin and R.G. Klein (Tucson: University of Arizona Press, 1984), pp. 768–80. Some think Polynesians arrived in Hawaii as early as the first century A.D. Matthew Spriggs and Atholl Anderson, "Late Colonization of East Polynesia," *Antiquity* 67 (1993): 200–217, review the literature and prefer a later date, ca. 600 to 950.

12. Harold Brookfield and John Overton, "How Old Is the Deforestation of Oceania?" in *Changing Tropical Forests,* ed. John Dargavel, Kay Dixon, and Noel Semple (Canberra: Centre for Resource and Envi-

ronmental Studies, Australian National University, 1988), pp. 89–102, 92–93, on Fiji. Dodson, *The Naive Lands*. Cheshire has much on Fiji, largely derived from W. Southern, "Environmental History of Fiji," Ph.D. dissertation, Australian National University, 1986. On New Zealand: M.S. McGlone, "Polynesian Deforestation in New Zealand: A Preliminary Synthesis," *Archaeology in Oceania* 18 (1983): 11–25; M.S. McGlone, "The Polynesian Settlement of New Zealand in Relation to Environmental and Biotic Changes," *New Zealand Journal of Ecology* 12 (1989), Supplement: 115–30; Atholl Anderson and Matt McGlone, "Living on the Edge: Prehistoric Land and People in New Zealand," in Dodson, *The Naive Lands*, pp. 199–241. Most of the forest destruction in New Zealand took place between the thirteenth and fifteenth centuries A.D. These forests had grown up between 15,000 and 9,000 years ago with the retreat of glaciers and climatic warming.

13. K.M. Nagata, "Early Plant Introductions in Hawai'i," *Hawaiian Journal of History* 19 (1985): 35–61; Cuddihy and Stone, *Native Hawaiian Vegetation*, pp. 31–32.

14. P.V. Kirch and Marshall Sahlins, *Anahulu: The Anthropology of History in the Kingdom of Hawaii*, 2 vols. (Chicago: University of Chicago Press, 1992), 2: 45–47, 168–69; P.V. Kirch, "The Impact of the Prehistoric Polynesians on the Hawaiian Ecosystem," *Pacific Science* 36 (1982): 1–14, 5, says Polynesians used all land below 500 meters that was neither arid nor cliffs. Kirch (*Polynesian Chiefdoms*, p. 123) states that "the Polynesians actively manipulated, modified, and at times degraded their island habitats, producing ecological changes which were fraught with major consequences." Olson and James, *Fossil Avifauna of the Hawaiian Islands*, p. 777, say, "By removing [lowland forest] habitats from the Hawaiian Islands, the Polynesians wrought a greater change in the total biota of the archipelago than has been accomplished by all post-European inroads in the wet montane forests."

15. Brookfield and Overton, "Deforestation of Oceania?" pp. 92–93. These swamps may also have improved conditions for anopheline mosquitoes, the vector for malaria. I know of no evidence concerning malaria in prehistoric Melanesia, but it is possible that its role varied with landscape changes effected by humankind. This was true on another frontier of the malarial domain, the Mediterranean world.

16. Anderson and McGlone, "Living on the Edge," pp. 221–22.

17. Kirch, "Hawaiian Ecosystem"; Kirch, *Polynesian Chiefdoms*, p. 139; Fosberg, "Society Islands," p. 236. In French Polynesia, the

forest service is planting pines on these fernlands. In some cases, such as Aneiytum Island in Vanuatu, erosion carried little cost to humans, because it transported soil from high ground to alluvial flats where it could be put to use. See Matthew Spriggs, "Prehistoric Man-Induced Landscape Enhancement in the Pacific: Examples and Limitations" in *Prehistoric Intensive Agriculture in the Tropics,* ed. I.S. Farrington (Oxford, UK: British Archaeological Reports, International Series 232, 1985), pt. I, pp. 409–34. P.V. Kirch, "Man's Role in Modifying Tropical and Subtropical Polynesian Ecosystems," *Archaeology in Oceania* 18 (1983): 26–31, found the same situation on Tikopia.

18. Gary A. Klee, "Oceania," in *World Systems of Traditional Resource Management,* ed. Gary A. Klee (London: Edward Arnold, 1980), pp. 245–81, 255.

19. Ibid., pp. 266–67.

20. Bahn and Flenley, *Easter Island,* pp. 164–80.

21. This is conventional wisdom. Spriggs and Anderson, "East Polynesia," suggest A.D. 650–900.

22. Roy A. Rappaport, "Aspects of Man's Influence upon Island Ecosystems: Alteration and Control," in *Man's Place in the Island Ecosystem,* ed. F.R. Fosberg, pp. 155–74 (Honolulu: Bishop Museum Press, 1963), p. 167.

23. See Kirch, *Polynesian Chiefdoms,* p. 98; O.A. Bushnell, *The Gifts of Civilization: Germs and Genocide in Hawaii* (Honolulu: University of Hawaii Press, 1993), pp. 5–6; David E. Stannard, *Before the Horror: The Population of Hawai'i on the Eve of Western Contact* (Honolulu: University of Hawaii Social Science Research Institute, 1989); and the symposium in *Pacific Studies* 13 (1990): 255–301. Estimates for Hawaiian population in 1778 vary from 100,000 to 1 million. For New Zealand, see McGlone, "Polynesian Settlement."

24. On "natural" environmental change, see Nunn, "Recent Environmental Changes"; Patrick D. Nunn, "Causes of Environmental Changes on Pacific Islands in the Last Millennium: Implications for Decision-Makers," in *Aspects of Environmental Change,* ed. T.R.R. Johnston and J.R. Flenley (Miscellaneous Series 91/1, Palmerston North: Massey University Department of Geography, 1991). On New Zealand erosion, see McGlone, "Polynesian Settlement"; B.G. McFadden, "Late Holocene Depositional Episodes in Coastal New Zealand," *New Zealand Journal of Ecology* 12 (1989), Supplement: 145–50; Patrick Grant, "Effects on New Zealand Vegetation of Late Holocene Ero-

sion and Alluvial Sedimentation," *New Zealand Journal of Ecology* 12 (1989), Supplement: 131–44; M.J. McSaveny and Ian E. Whitehouse, "Anthropic Erosion of Mountain Land in Canterbury," *New Zealand Journal of Ecology* 12 (1989), Supplement: 151–64. I put "natural" in quotation marks because of the conflict between the conventional (and useful) distinction between human and nonhuman agency, and the fact that human beings are part of nature.

25. Carlos Prieto, *El Oceano pacifico: Navigantes españoles del siglo XVI.* (Barcelona: Alianza, 1975), 93–97; O.H.K. Spate, *The Pacific Since Magellan,* 3 vols. (Minneapolis: University of Minnesota Press, 1979–88), 1:128–29, 3:56–58, 208; Elmer Drew Merrill, "The Botany of Cook's Voyages, and Its Unexpected Significance in Relation to Anthropology, Biogeography, and History," *Chronica Botanica* 14, no. 5–6 (1954): 161–384, 239. Guam had perhaps 50,000 people before the Jesuit mission; about 4,000 in 1710. By 1786, only 1,318 Chamorros remained, but 2,626 were counted in 1810. After that, counts did not distinguish Chamorros from others in Guam. See Spate, *Pacific Since Magellan,* 2:115–18.

26. Pablo Guzman-Rivas, "Reciprocal Geographic Influences of the Trans-Pacific Galleon Trade," Ph.D. dissertation, University of Texas, 1960, pp. 92–133, 195–208, discusses the biological exchange between the Americas and the Philippines. Many American plants, including maize, potato, and cassava, were transported westward across the ocean, while few went the other way. Not until Cook suggested the idea to the British Admiralty did Pacific Island breadfruit make its voyage to the Caribbean in care of Captain Bligh. Merrill, "Botany of Cook's Voyages," p. 230 and passim, argues that most exotic weeds in the Philippines were introduced from Mexico and Brazil to the East Indies via Portuguese routes from Brazil to Goa in the sixteenth century. This might have meant an early introduction of American plants to Guam, but that is by no means clear. Traffic from the Philippines to Guam (as opposed to the reverse) was light. By 1914, 20 percent of Guam's flora were American species, mostly from Mexico and Brazil. Ibid., p. 237. An exception to the rule of ecological stability before Cook's arrival is the uninhabited Juan Fernandez Islands. Spanish mariners introduced alien species and effected a biotic revolution there between 1574 and 1750. See Lyndon Wester, "Invasions and Extinctions on Masatierra (Juan Fernandez Islands): A Review of Early Historical Evidence," *Journal of Historical Geography* 17 (1991): 18–34. In this respect, these islands parallel the Madeiras, uninhabited before the

fifteenth century and profoundly altered by species and fire brought by Portuguese mariners. Alexander Selkirk, prototype for Daniel Defoe's Robinson Crusoe, was marooned in the Juan Fernandez Islands early in the eighteenth century.

27. J.L. Rallu, *Les populations océaniennes aux XIXe et XXe siècles* (Paris: INED, 1990).

28. Bushnell, *Gifts of Civilization*, p. 295.

29. A historian who considers the depopulation of the Pacific islands myth or wild exaggeration is K.R. Howe, *Where the Waves Fall: A New South Sea Islands History from the First Settlement to Colonial Rule* (Sydney: Allen and Unwin, 1984). This, I think, is a mistake born of Howe's sympathetic effort to portray Pacific Islanders not as playthings of fate but as actors deciding their own destinies. Howe perhaps reacted to the "Fatal Impact" school of Pacific historiography, exemplified in Alan Moorehead's book of that title.

30. Ian Pool, *Te imi Maori* (Auckland: University of Auckland Press, 1991).

31. Bushnell, *Gifts of Civilization,* p. 211.

32. Rallu, *Les populations océaniennes,* p. 336.

33. Charles Wilkes, *Narrative of the United States Exploring Expedition during the Years 1838, 1839, 1840, 1841, 1842,* 5 vols. (Upper Saddle River, NJ: Gregg Press, 1970 [1845]), 3: 32.

34. Brookfield and Overton, "Deforestation of Oceania?" p. 91.

35. Nunn, "Recent Environmental Changes," p. 133.

36. Kirch and Sahlins, *Anahulu,* 2:169–70; Cuddihy and Stone, "Alteration of Hawaiian Vegetation," pp. 40, 53–57; Matthew Spriggs, "Preceded by Forest: Changing Interpretations of Landscape Change on Koho'olawe," *Asian Perspectives* 30 (1991): 71–116. The impact on native plants of introduced grazing and browsing mammals is still strong. Wild horses are destroying vegetation in the Marquesas, especially Nuka Hiva; deer and opossums are chewing away at New Zealand forests.

37. M. Laird, "Overview and Perspectives," in *Commerce and the Spread of Pests and Disease Vectors,* ed. Marshall Laird (New York: Praeger, 1984), pp. 291–325. Bushnell, *Gifts of Civilization,* pp. 50–51, believes *A. aegypti* (or else *A. S. albopictus*) must have been present by 1852. Yellow fever, borne by the same mosquito, has never established itself in the Pacific, for reasons that confound the medical profession. Hawaii lacks *Anopheles* mosquitoes, and hence malaria, which has long been deadly in Melanesia.

38. Herman Melville on rats aboard whaling ships: "They stood in their holes peering at you like old grandfathers in a doorway. Often they darted in upon us at meal times and nibbled our food . . . every chink and cranny swarmed with them; they did not live among you, but you among them." Quoted in Carolyn King, *Immigrant Killers: Introduced Predators and the Conservation of Birds in New Zealand* (Auckland: Oxford University Press, 1984), p. 68. Two healthy rats in three years might generate 20 million descendants; in ten years, if all went well—it never does—they could produce 5 x 10^{17} (50 quadrillion) progeny. See Joan Druett, *Exotic Intruders: The Introduction of Plants and Animals into New Zealand* (Auckland: Heinemann, 1983), p. 213.

39. King, *Immigrant Killers,* pp. 55–56.

40. Innovations in question were the steam-powered catcher boat (which could chase the fastest whales), the mounted harpoon gun with explosive harpoons, and pumps that inflated dead rorquals (which otherwise sink), allowing whalers to process them at sea. The rise of petroleum as fuel and lubricant also reduced the commercial viability of whaling after 1860. Baleen prices remained high.

41. Cuddihy and Stone, "Alteration of Hawaiian Vegetation," p. 38.

42. R.G. Ward, "The Pacific Bêche-de-mer Trade with Special Reference to Fiji," in *Man in the Pacific: Essays on Geographical Change in the Pacific Islands,* ed. R.G. Ward (Oxford, UK: Clarendon Press, 1972), pp. 91–123.

43. Ibid., pp. 117–18.

44. Dorothy Shineberg, *They Came for Sandalwood: A Study of the Sandalwood Trade of the South-West Pacific, 1830–65* (Melbourne: University of Melbourne Press, 1967); Mark Merlin and Dan VanRavensway, "The History of Human Impact on the Genus *Santalum* in Hawai'i," in *Proceedings of the Symposium on Sandalwood in the Pacific* (Berkeley: U.S. Forest Service Pacific Southwest Research Station, 1990), pp. 46–60; Kirch and Sahlins, *Anahulu,* 1: 57–97; Sonia Juvik and James O. Juvik, "Images and Valuations of Hawaiian Rainforests: An Historical Perspective," in *Changing Tropical Forests,* ed. John Dargavel, Kay Dixon, and Noel Semple, (Canberra: Centre for Resource and Environmental Studies, Australian National University, 1988), pp. 377–92, 381; Cuddihy and Stone, "Alter-

ation of Hawaiian Vegetation," pp. 39, 58. The trade was revived in Hawaii in 1988: the last stands of mature sandalwood were converted into a profit of either $40,000 or $1 million, depending on whom one believes.

45. Cuddihy and Stone, "Alteration of Hawaiian Vegetation," pp. 45–47.

46. Aristotle *Politics* 2.3; F.R. Fosberg, "Past, Present, and Future Conservation Problems of Oceanic Islands," in *Nature Conservation in the Pacific,* ed. A.B. Costin and R.H. Groves (Canberra: Australian National University Press, 1973), pp. 209–15; Klee, "Oceania," pp. 268–71; Garrett Hardin, "The Tragedy of the Commons," *Science* 162 (1968): 1243–48.

47. This chronology does not hold well for New Zealand, where environmental change peaked in the century after British settlement (1840–1940) and the China trade mattered little. But even here the crescendo came after 1880.

48. An indication of the role of human transport in the dissemination of organisms is the speed at which influenza outbreaks traveled in the twentieth century. From early in the century until the late 1950s, they spread at the rate of ship and rail traffic; after the 1960s, at a rate determined by air transport. See J.M. Goldsmid, "The Introduction of Vectors and Disease into Australia: A Historical Perspective and Present-Day Threat," in Laird, *Commerce and the Spread of Pests,* pp. 177–207, 196.

49. Clipperton Island, for example, has always had a minimal biota, subject to sharp changes. Before the mid-nineteenth century it was uninhabited and covered with low forest. Then calamity befell it, probably a tropical storm, after which its open landscape was dominated by seabirds and land crabs. But between 1897 and 1917 phosphateers visited, and their pigs revolutionized the biota, feasting on birds and crabs. See Marie-Helene Sachet, "History of Change in the Biota of Clipperton Island," in *Pacific Basin Biogeography,* ed. J.L. Gressitt (Honolulu: Bishop Museum Press, 1963), pp. 525–34.

50. According to Alan Holt, "The Nature Conservancy, Honolulu," *The Economist,* April 10, 1993, pp. 91–92.

51. Ibid. He reports 30,000 per square kilometer, or 300 per hectare.

52. G.H. Rodda, T.H. Fritts, and P.J. Conry, "Origin and Population Growth of the Brown Tree Snake, *Boiga irregularis,* on Guam," *Pacific Science* 46 (1992): 46–57; Julie A. Savidge, "Extinction of an Island

Forest Avifauna by an Introduced Snake," *Ecology* 68 (1987): 660–68. Several snakes have made it to the Honolulu airport, but none farther. See *The Economist* 10 April 1993, pp. 91–92. Military aircraft may also have brought stowaway snakes.

53. The rabbits starved themselves into extinction, and vegetation recovered. See Nunn, "Recent Environmental Changes," p. 133. The sailing routes were France-Tahiti-New Caledonia; Australia-Solomons-Papua New Guinea; New Zealand-Tonga-Samoa-Fiji. See P.S. Dale and P.A. Maddison, "Transport Services as an Aid to Insect Dispersal in the South Pacific," in Laird, *Commerce and the Spread of Pests and Disease Vectors*, pp. 225–56, 244–50. Some human disease vectors spread too, such as the malaria-bearing *Anopheles* mosquito, which after 1945 colonized broad areas of the Pacific from bases in Southeast Asia and Melanesia (Laird, *Commerce and the Spread of Pests*, pp. 303–9). As yet, the malaria plasmodium has not become established in Polynesia or Micronesia. See Leslie B. Marshall, "Disease Ecologies of Australia and Oceania," in *The Cambridge World History of Human Disease*, ed. Kenneth F. Kiple (New York: Cambridge University Press, 1993), pp. 482–96, 485.

54. Mark R. Peattie, "The Nan'yo: Japan in the South Pacific, 1885–1945," in *The Japanese Colonial Empire, 1895–1945*, ed. Ramon H. Myers and Mark R. Peattie (Princeton: Princeton University Press, 1984), pp. 172–210, 192.

55. The intense fire regime associated with plantation agriculture and ranching has an effect upon ecosystems analogous to that of infectious disease. On its initial appearance it is highly destructive, but as it becomes endemic, it creates an ecosystem composed chiefly of species adapted to the effects of fire. Fiji, Hawaii, and much of the Pacific had to adjust to new disease and fire regimes between 1840 and 1950.

56. Paul W. Williams, "From Forest to Suburb: The Hydrological Impact of Man in New Zealand," in *The Land Our Future*, ed. A.G. Anderson (Auckland: Longman Paul, 1980), pp. 103–24; K.B. Cumberland, "Man in Nature in New Zealand," *New Zealand Geographer* 17 (1961): 37–54, 149–50.

57. Herbert Guthrie-Smith, a reflective man and a considerable naturalist, catalogued changes in the land on his Hawke's Bay sheep station (North Island): "Few sights are more engrossing, more enthralling,

than the play of wind and flame. . . . As a lover wraps his mistress in his arms, so the flames wrap the stately cabbage trees, stripping them naked of their matted mantles of brown, devouring their tall stems with kisses of fire. . . . Alas! that the run cannot once more be broken in . . . a fire on a dry day in a dry season is worth a ride of a thousand miles." Herbert Guthrie-Smith, *Tutira: The Story of a New Zealand Sheep Station* (Auckland: Reed, 1969 [1921]), p. 230. Even a man who lamented land degradation and loss of species enjoyed burning the forest.

58. Williams, "From Forest to Suburb," pp. 102–13. New Zealand is geologically young, and the climate is rainy and windy, so vegetation cover is crucial in limiting erosion. Major works on New Zealand erosion are Cumberland, "Man in Nature in New Zealand"; G.O. Eyles, "The Distribution and Severity of Present Soil Erosion in New Zealand," *New Zealand Geographer* 39 (1983): 12–28; L.W. McCaskill, *Hold This Land: A History of Soil Conservation in New Zealand* (Wellington: Reed and Reed, 1973); C.L. O'Laughlin and I.F. Owens, "Our Dynamic Environment," in *Southern Approaches: Geography in New Zealand,* ed. P.G. Holland and W.B. Johnston (Christchurch: New Zealand Geographical Society, 1987), pp. 59–90.

59. H.I. Manner, R.R. Thaman, and D.C. Hassall, "Plant Succession after Phosphate Mining on Nauru," *Australian Geographer* 16 (1985): 185–95. Vegetation does recover abandoned mining zones in Nauru. Initially 90 percent of species are exotics, but within decades native species colonize where there is soil. Even in this degraded environment, exotic species require continued disturbance, and absent that native species survive and flourish.

60. Philippe L. Hein, "Between Aldabra and Nauru," in *Sustainable Development and Environmental Management of Small Islands,* ed. W. Beller, P. d'Alaya, and Philippe Hein. *Man and the Biosphere Project,* vol. 5 (Paris: UNESCO and Parthenon, 1990); Barrie MacDonald and Maslyn Williams, *The Phosphateers* (Melbourne: Melbourne University Press, 1985), pp. 564–69; Andrew Mitchell, *A Fragile Paradise: Nature and Man in the Pacific* (London: Collins, 1989), pp. 26–31. Phosphate imports to Australia and New Zealand since 1920 have paralleled sheep numbers and meat production. High-pasture productivity depends on aerial topdressing with phosphates and superphosphates.

61. H.J. Wiens, *Atoll Environment and Ecology* (New Haven: Yale University Press, 1962), pp. 454–66.

62. Dale and Maddison, "Transport Services," p. 253. The pests included the German wasp and Australian soldierfly. New Zealanders also named an unwelcome weed Wild Irishman. It is curious how weeds acquire the names of unloved nationalities.

5

Helen Wheatley

Land and Agriculture in Australia

Coping with Change in a Fragile Environment

Culture and Agriculture

Of all human endeavors, agriculture is perhaps the most direct conversation that we have with nature. A farm is a cultural artifact of the relationship between humans and the Earth. Australian farming fits a European cultural pattern of settler colonialism with which most of us are intimately familiar, but it is also unique. The source of that uniqueness is the land itself, which challenged the Australians and constrained their ambitions.

This study of a twentieth-century encounter between Australians and Americans is based on two modern societies cut from the same cloth, both because of their British heritage and their settler colonial histories. They share similar histories, unfortunately, of exploitation and despoliation of the land. As the Australian saying goes, "If it moves, shoot it; if it doesn't, chop it down."[1] The people of both countries also shared a similar process of learning to differentiate between their inherited cultures and their own responses to their material circumstances—a process that, in both cases, became an important element of the discourse of nation building. In the United States, Frederick Jackson Turner's frontier thesis came to define this discourse, while in Australia scholars still debate the meanings and merits of the Bush Myth and the Australian Legend—a thesis that Australia derives its essential character from the personality of the rural working class.

Despite these similarities, there are important differences between the United States and Australia. Nationhood remains a problem for Australians. The theme of the 1988 Australian bicentennial was "to find a national identity," perhaps a sign that the descendants of the settlers have yet to come to terms with their land and with their place in the world. Australians express concern about their "cultural cringe," a maddening deference to the presumed cultural superiority of other Western cultures. Like many Latin Americans, Australians find world systems theory an apt description of their situation, describing Australia as a semiperipheral nation still caught in the grips of a colonial past. Geographer J.M. Powell describes his land as "the restive fringe,"[2] while literary critics Bob Hodge and Vijay Mishra assert that their colonial heritage gives Australians a "double vision" or "schizoid consciousness" that serves as "a primary marker of Australianness."[3]

These self-descriptions provide a useful basis for analyzing agriculture in Australia. By virtue of its settler colonial heritage, Australia is a very modern product of the world system. Australians strive to partake of and even to compete with the cultures and economies of Europe and the United States, but this effort inevitably reminds them of their limited resources and the persistence of their peripheral status. Australian "double vision," torn between the world and their peculiar place in it, seems to me to be an almost archetypal modern dilemma. It is not surprising that Australians often choose exploitative strategies to achieve their goals, which are defined by forces outside themselves and their environs.[4] What is most interesting is that sometimes Australians make an effort to reconcile their desires to the realities of climate and topography. In this case, I examine an encounter between Australians of a sheep and wheat region in the Northwest Plains of New South Wales (on the western side of the Dividing Range) and Western American farmers who came to Australia in the 1960s to grow cotton.

One important difference between Americans and Australians was that the United States was the more successful nation of the two. By the mid-twentieth century, Australians had developed enough knowledge about their environment and enough of a commitment to what we would now call "sustainability" to create a disjuncture between their view of the land and the view of the Americans, who introduced successfully new capital-intensive techniques of farming. The Americans challenged Australian ways of dealing with the land, and Australians were torn between the commercial appeal of cotton farming and their awareness of its dangers.

Cotton itself serves as an example of the contrasting histories of the two nations. Australians had flirted with cotton production before, but they had rejected the crop as undesirable in its social implications and unprofitable in a context of scarce labor, remote markets, and low prices.[5] An Australian interest in import substitution led to a subsidy system that allowed some cotton to persist in Queensland, but it was American success with mechanization and other advanced industrial technologies (especially irrigation and agrochemistry) that finally made cotton economically and culturally viable in Australia. In the span of two decades, Australia became one of the leading world exporters of cotton, and the crop has done much to help revive and expand the rural economies of Queensland and New South Wales.

Yet this success has come at a price. It has challenged Australian attitudes toward the land; it has strained that nation's relatively weak regulatory structure; and while the jury is still out on the ultimate effects of cotton farming on the land itself, the prognosis is far from promising. Now the scarcity of water, not of labor, lies at the heart of the problem.

Cotton and the Politics of Water

Water is a critical resource in rural Australia. The use that people make of scarce water can tell us something about their ethic of land use. The Australian Aborigines had strict rules to protect water holes for wildlife even during severe droughts.[6] Today, wildlife struggles for survival against an ethic in which water is claimed first by humans for their towns and for agriculture. In New South Wales important wetlands, the Macquarie Marches, have been severely diminished by agricultural activity. These wetlands in the midst of a semiarid landscape provide a habitat for waterfowl, some of them migratory. For decades, pastoralists seeking grazing land encroached on the wetlands, and in the 1960s the construction of a dam diminished them further. The state of New South Wales has set aside portions of the marshlands as a nature reserve and allocated a certain amount of water to provide for that wildlife. Aquatic life was also protected through the Fisheries and Oyster Farms Act, which made it illegal to impede the movement of fish. The dawning recognition of the importance of the wetlands has been undercut, however, by the arrival of a new and very thirsty rural industry along the Macquarie River: cotton farming.

Cotton production expanded into the Macquarie area in the 1980s, moving right onto the river flood plain. Both cotton and expanded pastoralism have changed the water regime, as farmers and graziers impound and divert the water, often illegally. The government of New South Wales has the institutional means to curb water use in order to preserve the marshlands, yet it has done very little.[7] Wildlife in agricultural areas has few organized defenders in Australia.[8]

In 1991, the people of New South Wales gained a new appreciation of the danger to inland river ecosystems when an outbreak of poisonous blue-green algae created a water-supply emergency on the Darling River. Years of reckless impoundment, diversion, overuse, and pollution of the Darling and other inland rivers, combined with a severe and prolonged drought, brought the river system to a state of collapse. One scientific specialist in the Department of Water Resources described the outbreak as the equivalent of a "massive heart attack" that demanded deep-seated reform.[9] Modification had caused the waters of the Darling to become slower moving, more turbid, warmer, often more saline, and more susceptible to eutrophication.

Although blue-green algae had been seen in the rivers during other dry spells, the outbreak in 1991 was the worst ever recorded. A tremendous expansion of cotton production, which brought aggressive development of water resources along numerous inland rivers, made cotton growers an obvious target of blame. As one elderly grazier put it, "If the cotton growers are letting stuff into the river and you're losing stock then they should lose their water license."[10]

Cotton growers denied that they were the main culprits in "letting stuff into the river," and government officials agreed. It seemed likely that sewage and stock raising were more responsible for the overload of nutrients (especially phosphates), if only because the thirsty cotton farmers were careful to conserve their own runoff. Selfish irrigators were threatened by the beefing up of water-licensing laws, but a narrow focus on the pollution issue evaded the broader problems of soil degradation, loss of vegetation, and impoundment and overuse of what had once been free-flowing rivers in a fragile ecosystem.

There is good reason to evade the larger implications of the 1991 crisis. Cotton is an important new rural industry. Since its establishment in the 1960s, it has brought new life to areas steeped in decline and depression, and it has expanded agriculture beyond its former boundaries, pushing deep into the rural fringe. "Back of Bourke" is a New South

Wales colloquialism for "way out in the sticks," yet the cotton economy has transformed Bourke into a thriving rural center by Australian standards.[11] For those who believe in rural development, cotton has been a ray of hope in an otherwise gloomy picture of steeply declining fortunes for sheep grazing, disappointing performance for cattle, and fierce competition with the Americans and Europeans on the international wheat market. Asian buyers like Australian cotton, and Australians have worked hard to meet the exacting standards of the international market.[12]

It is worth returning to the statement of the old grazier, however. "If [they] are letting stuff into the river and you're losing stock then they should lose their water license." His is not merely a pronouncement that polluters should be punished. It is a statement of values, reflecting decades of conflict between graziers and cotton farmers. Despite their usual role in Australian history of environmental villains, in the extreme world created by capital-intensive cotton farming, graziers almost stand for a land ethic based on sustainability, against the cotton growers' view that the environment can be altered successfully to meet the needs of intensive agriculture.[13]

The state and commonwealth governments had a history of supporting intensive agriculture in irrigated areas. When the American growers came to Australia, they were encouraged to set up their operations in government-sponsored projects, either in the Murrumbidgee Irrigation Area of New South Wales or the Ord River Irrigation Area in the remote northern tip of the state of Western Australia. The government viewed irrigated farming as an extremely risky proposition. Farmers should be encouraged to participate in government schemes in order to minimize their own risks and to benefit from the professional expertise and infrastructural support that only the government could afford to provide.

For the most part, Americans rejected these irrigation schemes. Government researchers knew less than they did, and the farmers disliked the prospect of government supervision. (Many had objected strongly to the terms of the U.S. Federal Reclamation Act and had resented the Single Variety Act in California, which forced them to grow only Acala cotton.)[14] Nor did the Americans favor the locations of the schemes. The Murrumbidgee scheme in New South Wales was too far south to provide an appropriate climate for the crop. The Ord River was too remote and had already shown evidence of severe problems with cotton. For these reasons, the Americans preferred the Namoi River basin in New South Wales. Irrigation could be provided by water impounded behind Keepit Dam.

Unlike the irrigation areas, the choice of the Namoi River put cotton growers into direct conflict with Australians who had already determined uses for both the land and the water. Independent sheep and wheat growers shared the area with leaseholding inhabitants of government-sponsored "soldier settlements" for war veterans.[15] To gain access to land, large cotton growers found it easiest to negotiate with the state officials who controlled the soldier settlement land. They obtained control over leaseholds by vaguely promising to train their legitimate possessors into the cotton business—an arrangement that immediately set off charges that the Americans were really just using dummies to control large illegal holdings.[16]

This was an accurate enough assessment, and violated the spirit of support for the smallholder that had marked Australian farm policy since its inception. Americans were well versed in bending similar intentions of their own government, such as the acreage limitations set for recipients of U.S. federal reclamation waters or income caps to federal farm subsidies.[17] On the other hand, graziers had a tradition themselves of taking advantage of ambiguities in the law.[18] The Country Party pushed for an end to soldier settler leaseholds in New South Wales, making this a very weak basis to challenge the cotton growers.

The state proved very lenient in granting water licenses as well. As soon as they were permitted to settle along the Namoi River, the cotton growers set out to dominate the water supply, gaining licenses for more water than was actually available.[19] State authorities were clearly unprepared for this level of demand, and local residents were astonished by the race to control land and water. While diversification was welcome, an American invasion was not. The Graziers Association of New South Wales put up a fairly strong political battle against the cotton industry, asserting that "the country still rests firmly on the sheep's back" and attempting to make an economic argument against "capital intensive patterns of land use," especially when cotton was protected from the full force of the market by tariffs, bounties, and now by water subsidies.[20] But the biggest complaint was that cotton irrigators used up all the water, leaving little and sometimes nothing to other license holders. Graziers found it necessary to form their own pressure group, the Lower Namoi Riparian Occupiers' Association, to counter the political strength of the cotton growers'

Namoi Water Users' Association. When a drought struck the area in the mid-1960s, cotton growers proved very selfish when confronted by the necessity of cooperating with a water-rationing plan.[21]

The struggle over the water held in Lake Keepit revealed a profound dissonance between the attitudes of rural Australians and the American interlopers. While the conflict was certainly a clash of political styles, with the Americans demonstrating great skill at organizing as an interest group, the fundamental conflict lay in attitudes toward the land. Most of the American immigrants came from California and Arizona. Their aggressive attitude was conditioned by the reliability of water supplies in the United States, and especially by their experience with federal reclamation programs such as California's Central Valley Project. Yet there is a huge difference between the geography of the American West and the geography of Australia. In the United States, immense mountain ranges provide a form of water storage that, with massive intervention, can even out climatic fluctuations between wet years and dry years. In northern New South Wales, annual fluctuations of climate cannot be easily remedied.

Keepit Dam itself was the result of decades of effort on the part of local farmers and graziers to persuade the government to provide a supplement to groundwater. The New South Wales government, ever reluctant to expend precious capital resources, had started the dam in 1940 but postponed the work during the war and after because the Water Conservation and Irrigation Commission successfully implemented a groundwater improvement and conservation program. The dam was finally completed in 1959, but did not hold enough water to justify creating a government irrigation scheme.[22] The arrival of the Americans promised to transform a white elephant into a developers' dream, but where cotton farmers and the New South Wales government saw a wonderful, underused reservoir for holding irrigation water, the locals saw a hard-won safeguard against drought and devastating floods. Both the drought and later floods caught the Americans by surprise, whereas the locals understood that the climate was extremely variable and unpredictable. Cotton growers did not understand the cautious and frugal attitude of the graziers, whose risk-avoidance strategies were conditioned by experience. This conflict emerged very directly in a debate over how to manage Lake Keepit. Cotton farmers wanted to fill it to maximum capacity during wet years, whereas graziers wanted to keep it below the maximum in order to provide against the danger of flood waters.[23]

During the drought in the mid-1960s, graziers also expressed concern that groundwater supplies would be affected by cotton production. Government hydrologists assured them, unwisely, that their fears were unfounded. As the drought continued, over 150 miles of the Namoi River downstream from the cotton farms dried up. Graziers turned to their water pumps, only to find that, in some areas, the superior capacity of the cotton growers' wide-bore pumps had drained the water table below the level of the graziers' more modest pumps. Like the big Buicks that seemed to characterize the new American farmers in their midst, these powerful pumps represented a new level of very conspicuous consumption.

When one grazier, Don McCredie, attempted to get information about the size of the pumps being installed by the cotton growers, he found that "the Yanks have suddenly 'shut up' because they realize their already wide unpopularity is further deteriorating." Rumor had it that a team of Texas drillers had arrived with a rig that could drill up to 3,000 feet—and that the Texans had received a subsidy from the New South Wales government to transport the rig. Graziers feared the loss of their herds, which would take years to build up again, and resented what they felt was government favoritism toward the cotton growers. As McCredie wrote to a colleague,

> I have no objection to irrigation from bores by *anyone* provided that such extraction of water is in the best long term interest of Australia for Australians (and British immigrants also) and that such extraction of water does not in any way jeopardize the current form of production in any area or increase the costs of production in that area (i.e., That by too much irrigation pumping other primary producers find the water levels dropping in their bores and so they have to get boring contractors in and DEEPEN their stock and domestic bores and put in motors [instead of windmills] to draw the water from the greater depths.) My trouble is I'm one brought up as conscious of value for conservation for long term security—not conservation for short term reckless EXPLOITATION.[24]

The cotton growers ultimately won the argument in the Namoi River area because they outperformed the graziers economically, and because graziers did not find a way to pressure the state to regulate the cotton growers. Even when subsidies to cotton production were discontinued, the industry took hold and expanded into new areas. The relatively small scale of water-development projects in New South Wales and Queensland enabled cotton farmers, many of them Australian by this time, to band together and create their own financing plans, reducing the regulatory influence of government still further. The growers became more skilled both at negotiation and at using the available resources, but the question of long-term sustainability remained unresolved, as we have seen with the complex threat to the Darling River.

Land Use and Cultural Values

The challenge of the cotton growers may point to a classic instance of technological diffusion raising questions of appropriate versus inappropriate technology. The Americans developed their capital-intensive, irrigated agricultural techniques in the unique context of seemingly plentiful resources and extremely generous state subsidies. They transplanted that system to a country of very scarce and unreliable natural and capital resources, where the struggle over water control could be a zero-sum game and where the state had less patronage to dispense. Graziers had adjusted to these Australian facts of life by following a conservative strategy that they hoped would strain neither the land nor the patience of the state too much. They had ample historical support for their view that, with the exception of some specific areas where climate, geography, and infrastructure made intensive agriculture possible, rural Australia was best served by pastoralism and by extensive forms of farming such as wheat growing. This was what they meant when they asserted that the country still rode "on the sheep's back."

Yet the similarities between the Australians and the Americans were greater than their differences. J.M. Powell describes the pastoral ethic as one based on "the self-made, supremely independent man; [a] ubiquitous profit-orientation, whether in land or livestock; a contempt for remote and supposedly unsympathetic governments; a penchant for speculation, producing short-term gains by exploiting every economic and environmental windfall; extreme reluctance to adopt known conservation practices; the display of elaborate skills in the quest for financial and other forms of government relief"[25]—in short, the very character displayed by the immigrant cotton farmers.

Here we return to the paradox of rural Australia. Both graziers and cotton farmers extract their living from the land, engaged, as I suggested at the start, in an intimate dialogue with nature. Yet they do so as participants in a global network of relations that is far removed from the land. Here again, we find ourselves pondering Australian double vision.

The unwholesome reputation of the pastoralist, as described by Powell, marks him in traditional Australian iconography as a creature of empire, rather than a native son of the soil. Yet the sheep raisers can be seen in another light, as the realists who recognized the true nature of the Australian interior and found the best way to exploit it, while armchair theorists wove their dangerous fantasies of a nation blanketed by sturdy yeoman farmers. True, theirs was an imperial undertaking, but it was also quintessentially Australian.

The agricultural revolution of the twentieth century suggested the possibility that rural Australia might be freed from the limitations of place that had given graziers their peculiar prominence. Defined by its reliance on inputs, capital-intensive agriculture such as cotton production is based on the idea that land and agricultural practices can be fit to universal models set by the industry. To the degree that rural Australians retain their orientation toward the world market, the wholesale alteration of the landscape to produce cotton according to these universal standards is entirely consistent with Australian attitudes toward nature. For a settler colonial people, the "sense of place" was missing from the start, and the environmental dangers inherent in commercial agriculture were almost beside the point.

As Australian geographer Ken Johnson puts it, "Australia is a place poorly appreciated by its people," most of whom live in coastal cities. "Our economy is dominated by commercial and capital interests," he says. Yet, as a follower rather than a leader of that world economy, Australia suffers the exaggerated effects that swings in that economy can produce in what he calls a "small semi-peripheral country."[26] For rural people already coping with an unusually variable climate and a relatively poor environment, the grazier's opportunistic character remains a rational strategy: make the best of the good times, to ride through the bad times.

The irrigators on the inland rivers know that the threat of salinization looms before them, on top of all the other problems with the use of and competition over water resources. Australians in general are now aware of the threat to their river systems. Some, like the graziers of the Namoi River, now grope toward a way of living *with* the land, rather than despite it. Crisis has forced them to acknowledge their own experience with the land. Their double vision is drawn for a moment to what is underfoot, rather than on the horizon. A newfound respect for Aboriginal practices, an increasingly sophisticated and scientific understanding of the land,[27] a new interest in the potential use values of native flora and fauna, and even a bold effort to forge a new system of governance of the Murray-Darling basin[28] all reflect efforts by Euro-Australians to come to terms with their land. In 1989, Prime Minister Bob Hawke stood at the junction of the suffering Murray and Darling Rivers to proclaim the government's statement of the environment, *Our country our future.*[29] Our country? A brave statement for a "semi-peripheral" nation buffeted by the harsh winds of global markets. Australia's experience with cotton reveals to us a land of colonizers, grappling with the dilemmas of the colonized.

Notes

I wish to thank the Fulbright Foundation/Australian-American Educational Foundation for providing the opportunity to travel to Australia in 1991–1992, and the Australian National University for hosting me. Special thanks go to John Merritt.

1. Geoffrey Lawrence and Frank Vanclay, "Agricultural Changes in the Semiperiphery: Australia" in *The Global Restructuring of Agro-Food Systems,* ed. Philip McMichael (Ithaca, NY: Cornell University Press, 1994).

2. J.M. Powell, *An Historical Geography of Modern Australia: The Restive Fringe* (Cambridge, UK: Cambridge University Press, 1988).

3. Bob Hodge and Vijay Mishra, *The Dark Side of the Dream: Australian Literature and the Postcolonial Mind* (Sydney: Allen and Unwin, 1990), p. xvi. For an Australian exploration of the world sys-

tems theme, see Donald Denoon, *Settler Capitalism: The Dynamics of Dependent Development in the Southern Hemisphere* (Oxford, UK: Clarendon Press, 1983).

4. As Lawrence and Vanclay, "Agricultural Changes," explain, "The main spillover effects of short-term decision making imposed on farmers by the realities of the global marketplace have been declining rural incomes and severe ecological destruction."

5. Some cotton growers in Queensland enjoyed limited success with the crop, but an earlier government campaign to promote the crop had failed. I provide a fuller account of this first effort at introduction in my Ph.D. dissertation, "Power Farming: A Comparative History of Modern Cotton Production in the United States and Australia," Baltimore, Johns Hopkins University, 1993.

6. J.M. Powell, *Environmental Management in Australia, 1788–1914* (Oxford, UK: Oxford University Press, 1976), p. 9.

7. *The Australian Magazine* (weekend supplement to *The Australian*), May 16–17, 1992.

8. A relatively new environmental organization, the Inland Rivers Network, appears likely to be the most effective defender of the marshes, but until very recently the fate of the inland rivers was not as significant to the environmental movement as, for example, the depletion of the nation's forests.

9. *Sydney Morning Herald,* November 30, 1991.

10. *Sydney Morning Herald,* November 23, 1991.

11. Bourke (before cotton) is the subject of one of the earliest and best works of historical geography on New South Wales: R. Heathcote, *Back of Bourke, a Study of Land Appraisal and Settlement in Semi-arid Australia* (Melbourne: Melbourne University Press, 1961). On cotton, see Ross O'Shea, "The Cotton Industry at Bourke," *Australian Cotton Grower,* October 1982, pp. 6–7.

12. Australia is one of the top five cotton-exporting nations.

13. The irony of this situation should be clarified. In their study of the Murray-Darling Basin, Lawrence and Vanclay find that wheat cropping and grazing have led to severe consequences: "The soils of the basin are nutrient-deficient, then, and easily damaged by floods, droughts, and agricultural practices such as continuous cultivation. Increasing acidity and rising salty water tables are also severe problems. . . . Estimates of soil loss in 1988 were that for each metric ton of grain produced, some 13 metric tons were either blown or washed away.

Between 40 and 60 percent of farmers in the basin are considered to employ inadequate on-farm measures to combat soil erosion on their properties." (Lawrence and Vanclay, "Agricultural Changes"). These problems are steeply magnified by irrigated cotton production.

14. Pamela J. Merrill, "American Involvement and the Resurgence in the Australian Cotton Growing Industry, 1962–1972," Ph.D. dissertation, University of California, Berkeley, 1978. Merrill discusses a range of factors that induced Americans to resettle in Australia. See also Pamela J. Merrill and John J. Pigram, "American Involvement in the Australian Cotton Growing Industry, 1962–1972," *Australian Geographer* 16 (1984): 127–33.

15. For an introduction to the concept of soldier settlements in Australia, see Marilyn Lake, *The Limits of Hope: Soldier Settlement in Victoria, 1915–1935* (Melbourne: Oxford University Press, 1987).

16. In addition, the Americans were allowed to "jump the queue" in front of waiting settlers. At the time, foreigners were not allowed by law to take up that land. For some discussion of this issue, see the New South Wales *Parliamentary Debates,* 1963, 4253, 5872–73, and 8148.

17. J.J.J. Pigram, *The Development and Potential of the Namoi Valley Cotton Industry* (Armidale, New South Wales: Research Series in Applied Geography, no. 17., 1968).

18. Powell, *Environmental Management in Australia.*

19. Keepit Dam could store 100,000 acre feet of water, which meant that it could sustain 40,000 acres in cotton. Licenses had been granted for 90,000 acres of land. International Engineering Service Consortium, New South Wales Department of Conservation and Irrigation Commission, *An Economic Study of Keepit Dam, Northern New South Wales, Australia* (Sydney: Clarendon Press, 1969), p. 59.

20. Press Statement, September 21, 1966. E.H. Middleton, General Council of the Graziers' Association of New South Wales. Records of the Livestock Producers and Graziers Association. Butlin Archives of Business and Labor, Australian National University, Canberra.

21. Cotton growers saw the situation differently. "We are not adopting the attitude of 'I'm all right, Jack,' " insisted the chair of the Namoi Cotton Co-operative, John Howes. "The only income available in the Namoi Valley this year is from cotton." *Northern Daily Leader* (Tamworth), February 26, 1966. See also the issues for March 3 and 10, 1966.

22. International Engineering Service Consortium, *An Economic*

Study of Keepit Dam, 53. A useful account of many Australian water projects, including Keepit Dam, can be found in C.H. Munro, *Australian Water Resources and Their Development* (Sydney: Angus and Robertson, 1974).

23. The government itself failed to support this suggested use, arguing that the dam had been built for water conservation. A.H. Qilty, Water Conservation and Irrigation Commission: to Graziers, n.d. (April 1963). Records of the Livestock Producers and Graziers Association. Butlin Archives of Business and Labor, Australian National University, N9211893, Canberra.

24. McCredie to Fraser, August 12, 1966. Records of the Livestock Producers and Graziers Association, Butlin Archives of Business and Labor, Australian National University, Canberra.

25. Powell, *Historical Geography of Modern Australia.*

26. Ken Johnson, "Creating Place and Landscape," in *Australian Environmental History: Essays and Cases,* ed. Stephen Dovers (Oxford, UK: Oxford University Press, 1994), pp. 37–54.

27. Using water as an example, it is worth noting that even after World War II, planners had little useful hydrologic data on which to base decisions. See Munro, *Australian Water Resources.* To this day, groundwater resources have yet to be fully mapped. See the Australian Parliamentary Papers, *Water 2000: A Perspective on Australian Water Resources to the Year 2000* (Canberra: Australian Government Publishing Service, 1984).

28. See Peter Crabb, "Managing the Murray/Darling Basin," *Australian Geographer* 19, no. 1 (1988): 64–88.

29. Kevin Frawley, "Evolving Visions: Environmental Management and Nature Conservation in Australia," in Dovers, *Australian Environmental History,* pp. 55–78.

6

Valery J. Cholakov

Toward Eco-Revival?

The Cultural Roots of Russian Environmental Concerns

Throughout the 1970s many environmental concerns that originated in the 1960s in the West penetrated the Soviet bloc. For instance, Rachel Carson was published in translation in 1969, followed by others, such as Barry Commoner. While the official propaganda defined these environmental concerns as problems of the capitalist West, various dissenting movements in the East saw in them a chance to attack the system openly. Ecological consciousness spread among the peoples of Eastern Europe, and this contributed to the rise of civil discontent and the eventual downfall of the regimes.

This is a brief summary of recent events, but while it is true that the first protests against the governments were indeed environmentally motivated (e.g., "eco-*glasnost*"), the roots of environmental concerns in this part of the world are much deeper. In fact, I argue that environmental conscious-ness in Russia and Eastern Europe has a long tradition and that there are several identifiable stages in a process of growing environmental awareness, each related to a partic-ular epoch and a specific set of problems. Basically, as elsewhere in the world, the rise of environmentalism in Eastern Europe reflected the growth of modern industrial and agrarian economies and the increase in population.

The State and the Nobles

The earliest measures to protect the environment were linked to the interests of the state, the major actor in East European societies. In the seventeenth century, Tsar Alexei of Muscovy forbade the cutting of the southern forests of Russia, because they were important for hindering the invasion of nomads from the steppe.[1] This is possibly a unique example of using environmental measures for military protection.

In the eighteenth century, Peter the Great took over the forests of Russia and tried to protect them for the needs of the navy.[2] This action was similar to what happened in Atlantic Europe (England, France, etc.) earlier. Actually, that such legislation was thought to be necessary even in forest-rich Russia shows that the danger of deforestation had already appeared.

Another event from the eighteenth century was the rise of landed estates in Russia. After 1761, the aristocrats were freed from state service, and many of them established countryside residential manors with surrounding parks. The initial model came from seventeenth-century Poland, but by the end of the eighteenth century architects and landscape architects from France, Italy, and other West European countries began working in Russia.[3]

These estates and parks became places where Nature was revered, protected, and managed. They also became oases for wildlife in an environment under the growing pressure of human population. The population of Russia was indeed growing rapidly. It doubled between 1850 and 1900. The land reform of 1861 divided the estates between the lords and the peasants. The parks and the mansions were preserved, but the peasant lots dwindled, divided among numerous families.

Ideas about nature conservation and preservation came to Russia from Germany in the nineteenth century.[4] The tsarist government created some reserves for endangered species of economic importance (particularly fur-bearing animals). Wealthy individuals established private reserves. The idea of *Naturdenkmal* (*zapovednik,* or nature reserve) made its way. Along with this conservationism in the strict sense of the word, however, a more important development was taking place, which would have a far greater effect on Russia and its environment.

The Westernizers and the Slavophiles

During the Napoleonic Wars, the Russians encountered the West once again. To many, it was a shock. They realized that their country was backward and needed to catch up. Thus a movement began for modernization, whose adherents were called "westernizers." An unsuccessful revolt in 1825, however, put an end to their ascendancy for more than thirty years. During this time, another group predominated, emphasizing the uniqueness of Russia and its traditions. These were the so-called slavophiles. These two tendencies can be traced in earlier periods, but in the nineteenth century they turned into intellectual and political concepts.

After the humiliation of Russia in the Crimean War, the westernizers returned to power. The emancipation of the serfs came in 1861 and brought an increasing liberalization in society. In general, the 1860s were when the major trends in modern Russian thought got established. Among the upper classes, the old autocratic ideas coexisted with a newly accepted economic liberalism. The lower classes came to social life as well, since there were more opportunities for education and self-expression. Among these people of various origins, positivism made its impact, together with socialism.

These ideological movements produced certain attitudes and visions in regard to nature. The modernizers/westernizers wanted change in the European fashion. The government relied on liberal capitalism, at least in the beginning. The radicals also relied on individual action—they believed that by going to the countryside to work as teachers, doctors, and the like, they would enlighten the common folk and bring about change.

In the 1870s, there was change indeed. The government became more and more interventionist, and the radicals turned to political action. The slavophiles developed the concept of panslavism, which led Russia on a collision course with its neighbors. In the 1880s, the government began to build a network of railroads, culminating with the Trans-Siberian Railroad in the 1890s.[5] The radicals also evolved from their scientistic beliefs into a conviction that they must change society first.

Thus, by the end of the nineteenth century, one could see the following picture: westernizers wanted to make Russia similar to the rest of Europe whether through liberal legislation, government intervention, or revolutionary change. Basically they wanted to apply Western science and technology and to overcome the different obstacles on the way to this goal. The change, once achieved, would lead to betterment of the Russian economy, or private fortunes, or the masses.

On the other side were those who believed that the whole idea of change and progress was put incorrectly. The traditionalists believed that Russia must preserve its special social structure—the autocracy. This was a social pyramid ultimately rooted in the village commune. The village commune was the anchor also for the socialists evolving toward anarchism. They believed in the preservation of the commune after the hierarchies were dismantled.

All sides in this controversy placed humans, not nature, at the center of the discussion.[6] Whether they lived a traditional rural life or went to conquer new lands and establish new ways of life, they believed that nature was to serve them. Therefore, all this development, traditional or radical, existed within an anthropocentric view of nature.

By the end of the century, however, small groups of ecocentric voices appeared. These were either naturalists or poets and writers who found an intrinsic value in nature. It could be argued that this is a natural continuation of a traditional Russian regard for the land. It could also be seen as an outgrowth of the romantic worldview then in vogue among intellectuals. In times of utilitarianism, however, such views were difficult to defend and were not very popular in general. Usually they were either disguised or mixed with other concepts. Now, with hindsight, one can read the old authors in a more ecological way and find that their views were a complex mixture of different concepts.[7]

The Tradition of the Protection of Nature

Beginning in the 1850s, the Russians became aware of the geographical particularity of their country.[8] They began to seek in geography the explanation of their history and their backwardness. The "geographical factor" has played an important role in Russian culture ever since. This developed along two rather contradictory lines. On the one hand, grandiose projects to change nature emerged up to the 1980s; on the other hand, the importance of the geographical factor was downplayed, and the priority of social change was emphasized.

All the cultural and ideological diversity created during the nineteenth century can be traced in the twentieth century in the various discourses in Russia and Eastern Europe, and in Western scholarship dealing with that part of the world. Thus, the attitudes toward nature found in contemporary ideological rhetorics may point to the origins of the different visions of the man/nature relation in earlier periods.

The first reserves for fur animals were established early in this century. This was part of the overall conservation movement in many countries at that time, including the United States. Support for conservation persisted even during the civil war in Russia. The peasants who took over the estates of the big landlords threatened also to take over the few existing reserves. The Bolshevik government prevented that and established more reserves. This is sometimes credited to Lenin personally, who is believed to have acquired a liking for mountains while in exile in Switzerland.[9] A more plausible explanation could be that the state gave land to the peasants reluctantly and tried to keep some for itself in the form of nature reserves. Also, the idea that reserves are important in the long-term state interest was already established to some extent in Russia. No doubt examples from other countries helped to support this view.

It was difficult, however, to sustain an attitude protective of nature in a society like the early Soviet Union. All land was supposed to serve the people and be "productive." The idea of locking away some territory for the sake of animals and plants was declared a bourgeois attempt to prevent the working masses from getting to the land for recreation or more direct use. Powerful positions in the bureaucracy were increasingly held by self-termed "creative biologists" who wanted the reserves, not to remain intact for the scientific observation of nature, but turned into experimental stations for the acclimatization of new species and for breeding new, more productive varieties.

To this the naturalists answered that only after studying life in an undisturbed condition would it be possible to find out more about its mechanisms and gain the scientific knowledge needed to achieve command over life processes. Only then would it be possible, ran this argument, to modify life for more productive ends. By the late 1920s, this sort of reasoning was wearing thin the patience of the Soviet government, which wanted results in the economy quickly. The antiprotectionist group joined power with the rising group of Lysenkoite agronomers (Trofim Lysenko was a Stalinist bureaucrat who suppressed Mendelian genetics, Darwinian evolutionary biology, and conservationist ecology) and managed to take over the Ministry of Agriculture. In this way they gained control over 99.5 percent of Soviet territory. Thus the battle for control over the reserves lost its immediacy for the antiprotectionists for another twenty years.[10]

The Stalinist Period: Man as Transformer of Nature

By the end of the 1940s, "land hunger" developed in the Soviet Union, and suddenly the territory of the reserves was diminished drastically. Stalinist planners and engineers developed giant projects for turning rivers around and making deserts into gardens. Thus, for example, a huge project was promoted to create a giant lake in western Siberia, draining to the south into the Aral and Caspian Seas. A territory of 250,000 square kilometers was to be inundated.[11] Such was the scale of Stalin's plan for the transformation of nature. Projects of this sort were abandoned only in the mid-1980s. Meanwhile, a lot of smaller schemes were carried out. The Soviet Ministry of Water Management had at its height in the early 1980s more than 2 million employees and was one of the largest economic organizations in history.

The Lake Baikal Case

By the end of the 1950s, the cause of environmental protection began to regain its position. Many nature reserves were restored to their former size, and new ones were established. A famous case for nature protection marks the period, which was a period of relative liberalization after Stalinism. By the late 1950s and early 1960s, projects to build cellulose factories and to increase the pace of logging around Lake Baikal began to be implemented. As it turned out, this cold and crystal-clear lake in central Siberia had a very fragile ecosystem. Negative changes were detected by biologists and soon opposition to the projects appeared.[12]

For the first time there was a large-scale discussion on nature protection in the mass press of the Soviet Union. The writer Sholokhov wrote in defense of "Holy Baikal" and against the "barbaric" attitude toward nature that seemed about to desecrate it. The dispute went on for many years. Even a film was made about it. Considering the nature of the former Soviet Union, such a public display of criticism deserves an explanation. One is still to be made. As a preliminary explanation, one could say that this was a relatively innocent case, which could be allowed to be heard in public without threatening the generally endorsed belief about the unproblematic state of nature in the Soviet Union. Indeed, the case was geographically localized to a region of little population and limited human industry. Thus an impression could be maintained that the pollution of Baikal was something exceptional in the Soviet Union.

Meanwhile, environmentalism was on the rise in the West. Books such as *Silent Spring* were translated, and the problems of pollution, limited resources, and global change came to broad attention. All this needed some sort of response by the official Soviet establishment. Indeed, by the mid-1970s a whole body of literature emerged, supported by previously little-known quotations from the classics of Marxism, maintaining that environmental problems were an inevitable part of the capitalist economy. Such problems could by definition not exist in a rationally planned central economy.

But beyond such crude economic arguments, the Russian and East European writers relied on a kind of thinking characteristic of such writers as Vladimir Vernadsky and Pierre Teilhard de Chardin. Vernadsky introduced the term "noosphere," or the sphere of reason, encompassing the area of rational human activity on the globe. The term was further developed by Teilhard in his *Phenomenon of Man*. In this philosophical picture, man appears as an agent of Reason and plays an organizing role on the planet.[13] This view fitted very well with the scientistic and technocratic beliefs that always have been part of Russian Marxist thought and later of the official Soviet ideology.

In the West, these stories of the rational Soviet stewardship of nature and the economy were never much accepted. Meanwhile, the Lake Baikal controversy was followed closely by Western environmentalists, and later other facts about environmental deterioration in the Soviet Union began to come to light. In the early 1970s, it became widely known that the Soviet Union had ecological problems just like every other industrialized country, if not worse. As we now know, it was much worse than anybody expected.

Environmental Problems in Russia and Eastern Europe

The reason for the magnitude of environmental problems in the former Soviet bloc is, ironically, exactly the allegedly rational system that the Soviet Union created and imposed also over Eastern Europe. The governments were well aware of the environmental problems and tried to find reasonable solutions. A large body of environmental laws and regulations appeared in almost every East European country. On paper, everything looked very nice. The reality was different.

While the Soviet Union and the other communist countries may have looked like monolithic, single-system societies, in fact there were diverse groups and interests under the ideological vestments woven by propaganda.[14] The Soviet government thought that it had to make a choice between having a cleaner environment and having more industry and military power; between preserving the resources of the country and the health of its citizens, on the one hand, and its aspirations for world power, on the other.

Information was always a carefully guarded state property in the Soviet Union. No news of any environmental deterioration could have leaked in the state-owned mass media unauthorized. At one point, even medical statistics, which could have indicated environmental deterioration through data on life expectancy and illness, were made secret.

Of course, this sort of governmental action was nothing new to the people. Like the subjects of other *ancien régimes*, they had an old tradition of relying on hearsay, in which typically the government policy of suppressing information only made things worse. The public, however, still had to be informed about environmental problems. This was done by another traditional method: the dissident network of circulation of manuscripts known as *samizdat* (self-published). A particularly striking example of this sort is the pamphlet *The Destruction of Nature in the Soviet Union*.[15] Its author used the pseudonym Boris Komarov and launched the manuscript in 1978. The book was published in English in 1980.

A very dark picture appeared on the pages of this book. The author talked about "secret land," "secret air," "secret water," and so forth, pointing to the cover-up of tremendous environmental catastrophe throughout the country. Some particular details indicated that the author was an informed Soviet specialist. (The author eventually managed to emigrate to Israel, where he now writes under the name of Ze'ev Wolfson.) The book was one of the few direct confirmations of the grave condition of nature in the Soviet Union.

The *perestroika* and *glasnost* periods, the attempt of the system to reform itself, which began in 1985, made it possible for the people of the Soviet Union and Eastern Europe to express their political concerns more openly. On many occasions, the dissidents began their public activity with protests against industrial pollution.[16] It was virtually impossible for the authorities to suppress such protest actions: on the one hand, there was the claim of ongoing liberalization; on the other hand, the protesters were not attacking the system directly but were expressing their concerns about something that was of importance to everybody—the environment.

By the late 1980s, a "green dissent" gathered momentum in Eastern Europe and the Soviet Union. The scale of the activity brought about their description as "green revolutions."[17] The downfall of the regimes, which began in 1989, made environmental information available to the public. What came out exceeded any anticipation. Some authors now speak about "ecocide" in the former Soviet Union.[18] Public discontent with pollution and environmental degradation fueled the emotions of the electorate in many places in Eastern Europe during the first free elections, which swept away the communist regimes.

Toward Eco-Revival in Russia and Eastern Europe?

Some time has already passed since the "green revolutions," and a continuation of the story can be written. The environmental concerns are still there. Nevertheless, many former communist countries find themselves among the poorer countries of this planet and cannot afford to clean up their environment. On many occasions polluting factories continue to operate because they provide jobs for an impoverished population. Bread has to come first, after all. Another observable fact is that the former dissenters are now mostly involved in party politics; they no longer need an environmental disguise to attack a system that has to be changed. Now they can do it openly by directly addressing issues of importance in social and political life. All this has led to the downscaling of environmental activism in Russia and Eastern Europe.[19] There are, however, positive developments in regard to the environment.

The gradual restructuring of the economy in Russia brought about the closure of many military industries, which were major polluters. The change in prices forced a more conserving attitude toward resources. Also in Russia, according to some observations, pollution has been concentrated in relatively small areas. There are still vast territories without much pollution.[20] All this brings hope that the environmental problems will stay localized and will slowly diminish even if Russia may not always have the technology or resources to clean up polluted areas.

In Eastern Europe, the environmental movements today resemble more closely those in the West. The people of Russia and the countries of Eastern Europe have environmental traditions that they can resurrect from previous times. "Protoecological" statements and ideas can be found particularly among authors who worked at the turn of the century or during the interwar period.[21]

As might be expected, considering the proximity of Western Europe and shared cultural traditions from the time before the Second World War, the East European countries have evolved along the lines of the existing green parties in the West, and ideologies representing a "green" version of nationalism have appeared. The same can be said as well about Russia, which shares, after all, much of its cultural tradition with the rest of Europe. But Russia is also a country of "pioneers" and "settlers" in its southern and eastern parts, which may bring about an environmental perspective in the study of its past and present similar to that of North America and Australia. Whatever the exact development, environmentalism has come to stay as an important part of culture, social life, and politics in Eastern Europe and Russia. Thus, although the 1980s Green movements in this part of the world may have represented political rather than environmental concerns, there are other reasons why these former communist countries can expect an eco-revival.

Notes

1. S.A. Demina, *Zakon na strazhe prirody* (Moscow, 1987), p. 63.
2. Douglas R. Weiner, *Models of Nature: Ecology, Conservation and Cultural Revolution in Soviet Russia* (Bloomington: Indiana University Press, 1988), p. 7.

3. *Energiia*, no. 4 (1989) (Moscow).

4. Weiner, *Models of Nature*, p. 11.

5. Steven G. Marks, *Road to Power: The Trans-Siberian Railroad and the Colonization of Asian Russia 1850–1917* (Ithaca, NY: Cornell University Press, 1991).

6. Donald R. Kelley et al., *The Economic Superpowers and the Environment: The United States, The Soviet Union and Japan* (San Francisco: W.H. Freeman, 1976), p. 23.

7. *Ekologicheskie intuitsii v russkoi kul'ture* (Moscow, 1992).

8. Sergei M. Solov'ev, *Istoriia Rossii s drevneishikh vremen*, vols. 1–29 (Moscow, 1851–1879).

9. Weiner, *Models of Nature*, p. 24.

10. Ibid., p. 228.

11. Philip Micklin, "The Falling Level of the Caspian Sea," in *Environmental Deterioration in the Soviet Union and Eastern Europe*, ed. Ivan Volgyes (New York: Praeger, 1974), p. 75.

12. G.I. Galaziy, "The Ecosystem of Lake Baikal and Problems of Environmental Protection," *Soviet Geography: Review and Translation* 22, no. 4 (1981): 217–25; Craig zum Brunnen, in Volgyes, *Environmental Deterioration*, p. 80.

13. Rudolf Balandin, *Planeta obretaet razum* (Moscow, 1970).

14. Charles E. Ziegler, *Environmental Policy in the USSR* (Amherst: University of Massachusetts Press, 1987), p. 46.

15. Boris Komarov, *The Destruction of Nature in the Soviet Union* (White Plains, NY: M.E. Sharpe, 1980).

16. Duncan Fisher, "The Emergence of the Environmental Movement in Eastern Europe and Its Role in the Revolutions of 1989," in *Environmental Action in Eastern Europe: Responses to Crisis*, ed. Barbara Jancar-Webster (Armonk, NY: M.E. Sharpe, 1993).

17. Hilary French, *Green Revolutions: Environmental Reconstruction in Eastern Europe and the Soviet Union*, Worldwatch Paper 99, November 1990.

18. Murray Feshbach and Alfred Friendly Jr., *Ecocide in the USSR* (New York: Basic Books, 1992).

19. D.J. Peterson, *Troubled Lands: The Legacy of Soviet Environmental Destruction* (Boulder, CO: Westview Press, 1993).

20. Ibid., p. 247.

21. *Ekologicheskie intuitsii v russkoi kul'ture* (Moscow, 1992).

7

Diane M. Jones

The Greening of Gandhi

Gandhian Thought and the Environmental Movement in India

The prominent environmentalist Anil Agarwal is fond of
affirming that in India, "environment is an idea whose time
has come." Indeed, environmentalism and environmental
action groups have proliferated in India over the past two
decades. With over 500 citizen groups advocating one form
or another of Green politics, India now has the largest environmental movement in Asia. Moreover, Indian environmentalism is having an impact well beyond the borders
of the subcontinent. The widely publicized Chipko movement with its tree-hugging strategy has provided inspiration
to forest preservation activists worldwide. More recently,
leading Indian environmentalists such as Vandana Shiva,
Madhav Gadgil, and Ramachandra Guha have become re-
spected voices in the world environmental movement.

Western environmentalism is certainly a major source of

inspiration for the growth of the Indian movement, but Indian environmentalists frequently cite another, indigenous, source of inspiration for their activities: the philosophy of Mahatma Gandhi. For them, Gandhi remains relevant not just as a prophet of nonviolence but also as the architect of a social vision that implicitly supports an environmental ethic. Many Indians and a few non-Indians have discovered in Gandhian philosophy the foundations for a "green mentality," described by Lloyd Rudolphs as "a mentality of self-mastery that lives at one with nature and fellow human beings."[1] Indian environmental leaders routinely invoke Gandhi's name when describing their own environmental philosophies, and India's small but still vital Gandhian movement has put a high priority on environmental concerns.[2]

At first glance, the identification of environmentalism and "Gandhism" is somewhat surprising, considering that in all his writings Gandhi made only a few references to the natural world and even fewer statements that could be taken as having specifically environmental import. The focus of his concern was almost exclusively social and political relationships among humans. One could even point to his fierce opposition to artificial birth control and his complacency about population growth as indicating a lack of environmental consciousness. And yet there lies within the Gandhian social vision an undercurrent of ecological awareness and conservatism that attracts Indian environmentalists today. This undercurrent seeps in and around the main pillars of the Gandhian social vision: asceticism and simple living; a rural-centered civilization based on village autonomy and self-sufficiency; handcrafts and manual labor; and the absence of exploitative economic relationships. One might say that environmentalism emerges from Gandhi's thought as a process of creative extrapolation, yet it is extrapolation that Gandhi himself might well have made had he lived longer.

The first purpose of this essay is, therefore, to demonstrate the sources for and the legitimacy of a "green" reading of Gandhi. Second, I propose to show how the Indian environmental movement[3] embodies important Gandhian principles, not only through its adoption of nonviolent techniques, but even more significantly in its embrace of Gandhian economic principles. One hears a distinct echo of Gandhi when Indian environmentalists defend traditional subsistence economies, advocate political and economic decentralization, criticize Western-style industrial development, and focus on overconsumption by the wealthy as an explanation of the roots of the environmental crisis. This orientation gives Indian environmentalism a unique quality and, to some extent, presents a philosophic challenge to environmentalists in the West.

Gandhism and Environmentalism

In searching for the environmental implications of Gandhi's thought, I have identified four ideas which facilitate a "green" rereading of his philosophy. The first and most fundamental was his insistence on the ancient Vedantic teaching that all life is ultimately one, a reflection of the divine. This idea underpinned his theory of nonviolence, or *ahimsa,* and constituted for him the "chief value" of Hinduism.[4] Moreover, it was in connection with this teaching that Gandhi made statements that transcended, rather uncharacteristically, the human frame of reference. He declared on one occasion:

> I want to realize brotherhood or identity not merely with the beings called human, but I want to realize identity with all life, even with such things as crawl upon earth ... because we claim descent from the same God. ... [5]

Gandhi found practical expressions of the principle of the oneness of creation in vegetarianism and cow worship. He defended the latter by arguing that cows should be honored as representatives of the whole of the animal kingdom.

A second fundamental principle of Gandhi's thought, again drawn from Hindu tradition, was asceticism. On one hand, Gandhi was undoubtedly attracted by the accepted notion that physical renunciation could lead toward spiritual enlightenment. But also, and more to the point, he argued that people must voluntarily limit consumption because there are upper limits to the bounty of nature. The environmental movement frequently quotes Gandhi to the effect that "There is enough in the world for everybody's need, but not for some people's greed." In Gandhi's view, voluntary poverty, or to put it more attractively, simple living, was not just for the spiritual seeker but an ecological imperative for all.

A third principle suggestive of a "green" interpretation of Gandhi was his outspoken opposition to exploitation. Gandhi condemned exploitation as the "essence of violence" and called for India to develop a "nonviolent" economy, that is, one free of exploitation. Gandhi explicitly associated exploitation with both colonialism and urbanization. And although he had in mind the exploitation of people by other people—of villages by cities and weak countries by strong countries—it is nonetheless tempting to extrapolate his views into a protest against exploitation of the earth. Given his conviction about the limitations on resources, Gandhi would probably not quarrel with this interpretation—and came close to it himself on at least one occasion:

> God forbid that India should ever take to industrialism after the manner of the West. The economic imperialism of a single tiny island kingdom (England) is today keeping the world in chains. If an entire nation of 300 million took to similar economic exploitation, it would strip the world bare like locusts.[6]

In fact, environmentalists Vandana Shiva and J. Bandopadhyay see in Gandhi's opposition to exploitation the roots of modern environmental consciousness in India:

> Gandhi's mobilization for a new society, where neither man nor nature is exploited and destroyed, was the beginning of this civilizational response to a threat to human survival.[7]

While these three principles—oneness of life, asceticism, and opposition to exploitation—all help to support a "green" reading of Gandhi, the most direct environmental implications of his thought are to be found in a fourth idea: the rejection of Western-style industrialization and modern machinery. He set out these views most systematically and forcibly in *Hind Swaraj,* or *Indian Home Rule,* published in 1908. Some present-day Gandhians regard *Hind Swaraj* as a visionary critique warning of the environmental problems that modern economic development would inevitably entail. In this polemical work, Gandhi attacked the "monster god of materialism"; he condemned modern Western civilization as "irreligion" and identified industrialization as its "chief symbol of evil." He argued that such modern conveniences as railroads undermine moral fiber and extend human power beyond its divinely ordained limitations. As such, they can only be a benefit to evildoers: "Railways accentuate the evil nature of man. Bad men fulfill their evil designs with greater rapidity."[8] He based further objections to industrialization on its exploitation of factory workers and destruction of traditional economies. Even the use of machinery by individuals leads to exploitation, he argued, for it allows people to amass land and wealth and thereby take advantage of their neighbors. Gandhi's ultimate argument in *Hind Swaraj* was that true self-rule would come to India only if Indians remained true to their own civilizational ways and rejected the ways of the modern West.

Although ridiculed by many of his contemporaries for such apparently obscurantist thinking, Gandhi never retreated from the basic thesis of *Hind Swaraj*. He devoted much of his life's work to creating an alternative, nonindustrial, village-centered economic development scheme for India and tried successfully to convince fellow nationalists that they should reject the European model of economic development. He exhorted them to abandon mechanization in favor of the spinning wheel, city life in favor of traditional village republics, and a strong central government in favor of local autonomy. At times, he modified his attack on machinery, saying that it should be condemned only when it robbed people of needed employment. Yet he continued to advise his followers to shun modern conveniences such as watches, fountain pens, and factory-made toothbrushes. He was apologetic about his own use of modern transport and maintained that his message was more effective when he traveled by foot or bullock cart. Ultimately, industrialization and the materialism it implied were simply incompatible with his vision of a spiritually based society:

> This land of ours was once, we are told, the abode of the gods. It is not possible to conceive of gods inhabiting a land which is made hideous by the smoke and the din of mill-chimneys and factories, and whose roadways are traversed by rushing engines, dragging numerous cars crowded with men who know not for the most part what they are after, who are often absent-minded, and whose tempers do not improve by being uncomfortably packed like sardines in boxes. . . . [9]

Gandhi took it on faith that there had been better times in the past, times when people lived more wisely and more comfortably. In that golden past, he asserted, "Nature did her work in her own way." The problem with modern technology is that "now we interfere with her work without full knowledge of her laws," with the result "that we are completely impoverished."[10]

Unfortunately for Gandhi, the educated mainstream of the Indian independence movement considered such ideas profoundly reactionary and unenlightened. After 1947, successive governments of free India attempted to take advantage of Gandhi's enormous prestige by invoking his memory at every turn, by decorating government offices and publications with his portrait. But in effect,

India's new leadership turned his picture to the wall as they pursued an economic development scheme that relied heavily on capital-intensive, large-scale, centralized, market-driven industrialization.

The Indian Environmental Movement and Gandhi

Over the past two decades, citizen-led environmental groups have organized around a multiplicity of causes and campaigns across the subcontinent. The most widely publicized struggles have been over issues of resource management: logging, mining, fishing, and dam building. In these struggles, environmental issues have often overlapped with and complemented issues of social justice. In less heavily populated countries, the impact of ecological destruction may be camouflaged for years, but in India it usually has a clear and immediate impact on some portion of the population. Since those affected are typically villagers living subsistence lifestyles and dependent on local ecosystems, Indian environmentalists have come to insist that "environmental degradation and social injustice are two sides of the same coin."[11] In the United States, environmental controversies often take the form of a contest between exploitation and preservation of natural resources. In India, the contest is more commonly between two competing modes of exploitation: capitalist/industrial versus traditional/subsistence.[12] The question ultimately is: who will have access to resources, corporations or villagers?

The most famous Indian environmental campaign, and one that illustrates this point, is the Chipko Movement. Begun in the mid-1970s—and as far as I know, still active—Chipko has also been called "one of the few viable manifestations in India of the Gandhian vision."[13] The famous strategy of people hugging trees in order to shield them from loggers was the inspiration of a Gandhian social worker, Chandi Prasad Bhatt, in 1973. Bhatt had been working for several years with villagers of the Himalayan region of Uttar Pradesh State to develop local self-help industries based on the small-scale harvest and processing of forest products. In 1973, when the government Department of Forestry refused to allow local villagers to cut a handful of ash trees for making tool handles but instead awarded the trees to an outside corporation for making tennis rackets, Bhatt and the villagers decided to take action. Following Bhatt's suggestion and displaying a Gandhian commitment to nonviolence and self-sacrifice, the villagers decided to hug the ash trees to protect them with their own bodies. They were successful, and "Chipko," which means "to cling to" or "to embrace," became the name for a movement that was to attract worldwide attention.

Bhatt took the strategy to other villages, and soon it was being used to obstruct logging for the purpose of environmental protection. Since the 1960s, the government had increased timber sales in the region, which, combined with widespread illegal cutting, had resulted in severe degradation of the watershed. The result had been a sharp increase in the incidence of disastrous floods and landslides in the region. At this point, village women began to participate vigorously in the movement and to emerge as Chipko leaders. Himalayan women, whose customary duties include gathering fuel and animal fodder, were more aware than the men of the hardships created by the progressive deterioration of the forest ecosystem. They found themselves walking farther and farther in search of the forest products on which they depended. Indeed, some observers maintain that the Chipko tactics were the idea of women in the first place.

The Chipko strategy proved successful on a number of occasions in the mid- and late 1970s and caught the attention of the nation. In 1981, negotiations between Chipko leaders and the government resulted in a fifteen-year moratorium on all cutting of green trees above 1,000 feet elevation. Since then, Chipko activists have been involved in environmental education, reforestation, and other activities. Meanwhile, within the movement itself, attitudes toward forest management have diverged. One point of view, represented by C.P. Bhatt, opposes large-scale commercial utilization by local groups. A second viewpoint, represented by another Gandhian social worker, Sunderlal Bahuguna, holds that forests should be protected from all commercial exploitation and that the products of a forest should be regarded as "soil, water and pure air." Bahuguna has conducted a number of Gandhi-like fasts and trans-Himalayan pilgrimages in defense of the forest and has emerged in India as the most charismatic Chipko leader. Like Gandhi, Bahuguna believes the ultimate problem is one of consumption:

> The ecological crisis in Himalaya . . . has its roots in the [modern] materialistic civilization which makes man the butcher of the earth.[14]

While Chipko is the best example of an environmental initiative movement with clear connections to Gandhian ideology, there appears to be a more general and wide-spread affinity between South Asian environmentalism and Gandhi's social vision. This affinity goes well beyond the fact that most environmental groups have adopted the technique of nonviolent protest and Gandhi's term for it, *satyagraha* (soul-force), to describe their actions. More strikingly, Indian environmentalists have breathed new life into Gandhi's much-maligned critique of Western-style industrialization and modernization. Like Gandhi, they advocate an alternative style of economic development that is oriented toward subsistence economies and traditional modes of production and that emphasizes equity over production of wealth. And, like Gandhi, they emphasize limitations on the Earth's resources and point to over-consumption—especially overconsumption by industrial-ized nations—as the main cause of environmental problems worldwide. Although it is an overstatement, there is some truth to the assertion that the contemporary environmental movement in India is "no more than a restatement of Mahatma Gandhi's vision of a decentralized economy based on agriculture and intermediate appropriate technology designed to meet the all-round social and economic needs of the rural poor."[15] James Rush, author of a recent study on Asian environmentalism, sizes up the movement in South Asia as nothing less than an attempt "to reverse the momentum of modern history."[16]

Environmentalists Ramachandra Guha and Madhav Gadgil state flatly that there is "no hope of emulating European or New World modes of industrial development" and call for both a "new mode of resource use" and a "new belief system" to go with it.[17] Likewise, Anil Agarwal suggests that with a proper approach to economic development India may become a "land of milk and honey for all" but not necessarily "a country of Hondas and IBM devices for all."[18] Guha, Gadgil, Agarwal, and others maintain that ecological prudence need not be the enemy of economic development but, on the contrary, a necessary precondition for rational and equitable development.[19] What is needed, in their view, is a new—and very Gandhian—style of development that would focus on rural areas, support subsistence economies, and emphasize local control over natural resources.

Indian environmentalists also display a Gandhian-style emphasis on the issue of consumption. They challenge what they see as the West's belief in unending material progress, especially as defined by greater and greater levels of consumption. Ramachandra Guha argues:

> The expansionist character of modern Western man will have to give way to an ethic of renunciation and self-limitation, in which spiritual and communal values play an increasing role in sustaining social life.[20]

Guha has even taken American environmentalists to task for failing to distance themselves from the culture of consumerism. This is reflected, he argues, in the American emphasis on wilderness preservation because "enjoyment of nature is an integral part of the consumer society."[21] By contrast, he praised the German Greens for advocating "no growth" economics and recognizing the necessity of scaling down current levels of consumption.

Indian environmentalists also join Gandhi in attacking market economics and upholding the value of subsistence lifestyles. Whereas Gandhi defended traditional subsistence economics on the basis of avoiding the kind of human exploitation that arises in a cash economy, Indian environmentalists defend subsistence lifestyles on the grounds that they are more ecologically benign. They argue that a market economy is inherently destructive because in interacting with nature it ignores and destroys nonmonetary assets such as watershed stabilization.[22]

Finally, Indian environmentalists often reiterate Gandhi's warning in *Hind Swaraj* about blind imitation of the West. They see the industrialized West as the main agent of environmental degradation because of its massive demand for natural resources, a demand that began in India during the colonial period. They regard the resource management policies of the present Indian government as nothing more than a continuation of the colonial pattern of exploitation. The intellectual challenge they can offer us in the West is that they draw important connections between environmentalism and social justice and suggest that on both counts we need to undertake a fundamental reevaluation of the economic and technological underpinnings of modern society.[23]

Notes

1. Lloyd I. Rudolph, "Contesting Civilizations: Gandhi and the Counter-Culture," *Gandhi Marg,* October–December 1990, 284–94.

2. As evidenced in the pages of *Gandhi Marg,* the journal of the New Delhi-based Gandhi Peace Foundation. It should be noted that modern environmentalists were not the first to put an explicitly environmental spin on Gandhi's notions about economic development. Writing in the 1930s through 1950s, two Gandhians, Pyarelal Nair and J.C. Kumarappa, placed strong emphasis on environmental concerns such as

soil fertility and opposition to chemical agriculture. See Pyarelal, *Gandhian Techniques in the Modern World* (Ahmedabad: Navajivan, 1953); and J.C. Kumarappa, *Economy of Permanence* (Varanasi: Sarva Seva Sangh Prakashan, 1946). Better known in the West is the British economist E.F. Schumacher, who in the 1960s and 1970s developed his notion of "Small is Beautiful" and the theory of environmentally sound "appropriate technology." Schumacher acknowledged Gandhian economics as one of the key sources of inspiration for his views. See E.F. Schumacher, *Small Is Beautiful: A Study of Economics As If People Mattered* (London: Abacus, 1973).

3. My generalizations about the Indian environmental movement are necessarily based on the writings of a handful of Indian environmentalists whose work is available in English.

4. Gandhi, *Collected Works,* 90 vols. (Delhi: Publications Division, Ministry of Information and Broadcasting, Government of India, 1958–), 64: 141.

5. Gandhi, *India of My Dreams* (Ahmedabad: Navajivan, 1952), pp. 14–15.

6. Jayanta Bandyopadhyay and Vandana Shiva, "Development, Poverty and the Growth of the Green Movement in India," *The Ecologist* 19, no. 3 (1989): 111–17.

7. Vandana Shiva and Jayanta Bandyopadhyay, "The Evolution, Structure and Impact of the Chipko Movement," *Mountain Research and Development* 6, no. 2 (1986): 133–42, 141.

8. Gandhi, *Collected Works,* 10: 21, 26, 37, 57–60.

9. Anand T. Hingorani, ed., *Socialism of My Conception* (Bombay: Bharatiya Vidya Bhavan, 1966).

10. Gandhi, *Collected Works,* 37: p. 38.

11. Anil Agarwal and Ravi Chopra, *The State of India's Environment: A Citizen's Report* (New Delhi: Centre for Science and Environment, 1985), p. 190.

12. Madhav Gadgil and Ramachandra Guha, *This Fissured Land: An Ecological History of India* (Berkeley and Los Angeles: University of California Press, 1993), pp. 244–45.

13. Gerald D. Berreman, "Chipko: A Movement to Save the Himalayan Environment and People," in *Contemporary Indian Tradition: Voices on Culture, Nature and the Challenge of Change,* ed. Carla M. Borden (Washington, DC, and London: Smithsonian Institution Press, 1989), p. 257.

14. Quoted in Ramachandra Guha, *The Unquiet Woods: Ecological Change and Peasant Resistance in the Himalaya* (Berkeley and Los Angeles: University of California Press, 1990), p. 179.

15. V. Kannath, "Review of Our Only Earth by Nagesh Hegde," in *Seminar* 355 (March 1989): 39.

16. James Rush, *The Last Tree: Reclaiming the Environment in Tropical Asia* (New York: Asia Society, 1991), p. 95.

17. Gadgil and Guha, *This Fissured Land,* p. 245.

18. Anil Agarwal, "Human-Nature Interactions in a Third World Country," *The Environmentalist* 6, no. 3 (Autumn 1986): 168.

19. Agarwal and Chopra, *State of India's Environment,* p. 190.

20. Ibid., p. 80. Similarly, Agarwal argues that the main source of environmental destruction in the world is demand for natural resources generated by the consumption of the rich. In Borden, *Contemporary Indian Tradition,* p. 273.

21. Agarwal and Chopra, *State of India's Environment,* p. 79.

22. Bandyopadhyay and Shiva, "Development of Green Movement in India," p. 115.

23. See Gadgil and Guha, *This Fissured Land.* See also Richard P. Tucker, "The Depletion of India's Forests under British Imperialism: Planters, Foresters, and Peasants in Assam and Kerala," in *The Ends of the Earth: Perspectives on Modern Environmental History,* ed. Donald Worster (Cambridge, UK: Cambridge University Press, 1988), pp. 118–40.

Selected Bibliography

This is a representative bibliography of writing on world environmental history, not a list of references for the chapters of this book. It should serve to give suggestions for further reading in the field. It does not pretend to be exhaustive, especially in North American environmental history, where the literature has become truly vast in recent years. The books listed here are environmental histories, studies of environmental history, and a few other works that are of importance to environmental historians.

1. On Environmental History

Cronon, William. "A Place for Stories: Nature, History, and Narrative." *Journal of American History* 78 (1992): 1347–76.

Crosby, Alfred W. "The Past and Present of Environmental History." *American Historical Review* 100 (1995): 1177–90.

Green, William A. "Environmental History," in *History, Historians, and the Dynamics of Change.* Westport, CT: Praeger, 1993, pp. 167–90.

Merchant, Carolyn, ed. *Ecology: Key Concepts in Critical Theory.* Atlantic Highlands, NJ: Humanities Press, 1994.

Simmons, Ian Gordon. *Environmental History: A Concise Introduction.* Oxford, UK: Blackwell, 1993.

2. Global in Scope

Bailes, Kendall E., ed. *Environmental History: Critical Issues in Comparative Perspective.* Lanham, MD: University Press of America, 1985.

Barbour, Ian, ed. *Western Man and Environmental Ethics: Attitudes toward Nature and Technology.* Reading, MA: Addison-Wesley, 1973.

Bilsky, Lester J., ed. *Historical Ecology: Essays on Environment and Social Change.* Port Washington, NY: Kennikat Press, 1980.

Crosby, Alfred W. *The Columbian Exchange: Biological and Cultural Consequences of 1492.* Westport, CT: Greenwood Press, 1972.

————. *Ecological Imperialism: The Biological Expansion of Europe, 900–1900.* Cambridge, UK: Cambridge University Press, 1986.

————. *Germs, Seeds, and Animals: Studies in Ecological History.* Armonk, NY: M.E. Sharpe, 1994.

Febvre, Lucien. *A Geographical Introduction to History.* New York: Knopf, 1925.

Griffiths, Tom, and Libby Robin, eds. *Ecology and Empire: Environmental History of Settler Societies.* Edinburgh: Keele University Press, 1997.

Grove, Richard H. *Green Imperialism: Colonial Expansion, Tropical Island Edens and the Origins of Environmentalism, 1600–1860.* Cambridge, UK: Cambridge University Press, 1995.

Huntington, Ellsworth. *Civilization and Climate.* New Haven: Yale University Press, 1927.

Ladurie, Emmanuel LeRoy. *Times of Feast, Times of Famine: A History of Climate Since the Year 1000.* Garden City, NY: Doubleday, 1967.

Marsh, George Perkins. *Man and Nature.* Cambridge: Harvard University Press, 1965 (1864).

McCormick, John. *Reclaiming Paradise: The Global Environmental Movement.* Bloomington: Indiana University Press, 1989.

Nash, Roderick F. *The Rights of Nature: A History of Environmental Ethics.* Madison: University of Wisconsin Press, 1989.

Ponting, Clive. *A Green History of the World.* New York: St. Martin's Press, 1991.

Pyne, Stephen J. *World Fire: The Culture of Fire on Earth.* New York: Holt, 1995.

Ramakrishnan, P.S., K.G. Saxena, and U.M. Chandrashekara, eds. *Conserving the Sacred.* Enfield, NH: Science Publishers, 1998.

Russell, William Moy Stratton. *Man, Nature, and History: Controlling the Environment.* New York: Natural History Press for the American Museum of Natural History, 1969.

Simmons, Ian Gordon. *Changing the Face of the Earth: Culture, Environment, History.* Oxford, UK: Blackwell, 1989.

Sponsel, Leslie E., Thomas N. Headland, and Robert C. Bailey, eds. *Tropical Deforestation: The Human Dimension.* New York: Columbia University Press, 1996.

Thomas, William L. Jr., ed. *Man's Role in Changing the Face of the Earth.* Chicago: University of Chicago Press, 1956.

Toynbee, Arnold. *Mankind and Mother Earth.* New York: Oxford University Press, 1976.

Tucker, Richard P., and John F. Richards, eds. *Global Deforestation and the Nineteenth-Century World Economy.* Durham: Duke University Press, 1983.

Turner, B.L. II et al., eds. *The Earth as Transformed by Human Action: Global and Regional Changes in the Biosphere over the Past 300 Years.* Cambridge, UK: Cambridge University Press, 1990.

Worster, Donald, ed. *The Ends of the Earth: Perspectives on Modern Environmental History.* Cambridge, UK: Cambridge University Press, 1988.

3. Asia

Arnold, David, and Ramachandra Guha. *Nature, Culture and Imperialism.* New Delhi: Oxford University Press, 1995.

Bandyopadhyay, Jayanta, and Vandana Shiva. "Development, Poverty and the Growth of the Green Movement in India." *The Ecologist* 19, no. 3 (1989): 111–17.

Chandran, M.D. Subash, and Madhav Gadgil. "Sacred Groves." *India International Centre Quarterly,* 1992: 183–99.

Gadgil, Madhav, and Ramachandra Guha. *This Fissured Land: An Ecological History of India.* Berkeley and Los Angeles: University of California Press, 1992.

Grove, Richard, Vinita Damodaran, and Satpal Sangwan, eds. *Nature and the Orient: Essays on the Environmental History of South and Southeast Asia.* Oxford, UK: Oxford University Press, 1995.

Guha, Ramachandra. *The Unquiet Woods: Ecological Change and Peasant Resistance in the Himalaya.* Berkeley and Los Angeles: University of California Press, 1990.

He Bochuan. *China on the Edge: The Crisis of Ecology and Development.* San Francisco: China Books and Periodicals, 1991.

Kumar, Deepak. *Science and the Raj, 1857–1905.* Delhi: Oxford University Press, 1995.

Rawat, Ajay S., ed. *History of Forestry in India.* New Delhi: Indus, 1991.

Shiva, Vandana, and Jayanta Bandyopadhyay. "The Evolution, Structure and Impact of the Chipko Movement," *Mountain Research and Development* 6, no. 2 (1986): 133–34.

Smil, Vaclav. *The Bad Earth: Environmental Degradation in China.* Armonk, NY: M.E. Sharpe, 1984.

Smith, T.C. *Agrarian Origins of Modern Japan.* New York: Atheneum, 1966.

Totman, Conrad. *The Green Archipelago: Forestry in Preindustrial Japan.* Berkeley and Los Angeles: University of California Press, 1989.

Tuan, Yi-Fu. *China.* Chicago: Aldine, 1969.

4. Europe and the Mediterranean

Bowlus, Charles R. "Ecological Crises in Fourteenth Century Europe." In *Historical Ecology: Essays on Environment and Social Change,* ed. Lester J. Bilsky, 86–99. Port Washington, NY: Kennikat Press, 1980.

Bratton, Susan Power. *Christianity, Wilderness, and Wildlife.* Scranton: University of Scranton Press, 1993.

Braudel, Fernand. *The Mediterranean and the Mediterranean World in the Age of Philip II.* New York: Harper and Row, 1972.

Brimblecombe, Peter, and Christian Pfister, eds. *The Silent Countdown: Essays in European Environmental History.* Berlin: Springer-Verlag, 1990.

Glacken, Clarence J. *Traces on the Rhodian Shore: Nature and Culture in Western Thought from Ancient Times to the End of the Eighteenth Century.* Berkeley and Los Angeles: University of California Press, 1967.

Hoffmann, Richard Charles. *Land, Liberties and Lordship in a Late Medieval Countryside: Agrarian Structures and Change in the Duchy of Wroclaw.* Philadephia: University of Pennsylvania Press, 1989.

―――. *Fishers' Craft and Lettered Art: Tracts on Fishing from the End of the Middle Ages.* Toronto: University of Toronto Press, 1997.

Hughes, J. Donald. *Ecology in Ancient Civilizations.* Albuquerque: University of New Mexico Press, 1975.

―――. "The Environmental Ethics of the Pythagoreans." *Environmental Ethics* 2 (Fall 1980): 195–213.

―――. *Pan's Travail: Environmental Problems of the Ancient Greeks and Romans.* Baltimore: Johns Hopkins University Press, 1994.

Jamison, Andrew, Ron Eyerman, and Jacqueline Cramer. *The Making of the New Environmental Consciousness: A Comparative Study of the Environmental Movements in Sweden, Denmark, and the Netherlands.* Edinburgh: Edinburgh University Press, 1990.

McNeill, John R. *The Mountains of the Mediterranean World: An Environmental History.* Cambridge, UK: Cambridge University Press, 1992.

Meiggs, Russell. *Trees and Timber in the Ancient Mediterranean World.* Oxford, UK: Clarendon Press, 1982.

Pyne, Stephen J. *Vestal Fire: An Environmental History, Told through Fire, of Europe and Europe's Encounter with the World.* Seattle: University of Washington Press, 1997.

Sallares, Robert. *The Ecology of the Ancient Greek World.* Ithaca, NY: Cornell University Press, 1991.

TeBrake, William. *Medieval Frontier: Culture and Ecology in Rijnland.* College Station: Texas A&M University Press, 1985.

Thirgood, J.V. *Man and the Mediterranean Forest.* London: Academic Press, 1981.

Weiner, Douglas R. "The Historical Origins of Soviet Environmentalism." *Environmental Review* 6, no. 2 (Fall 1982): 42–62.

―――. *Models of Nature: Ecology, Conservation, and Cultural Revolution in Soviet Russia.* Bloomington: Indiana University Press, 1988.

White, Lynn. "The Historical Roots of Our Ecologic Crisis." *Science* 155 (1967): 1203–7.

Worster, Donald. *Nature's Economy: A History of Ecological Ideas.* Cambridge, UK: Cambridge University Press, 1977. (History of ecological science in Britain and America.)

Ziegler, Charles E. *Environmental Policy in the USSR.* Amherst: University of Massachusetts Press, 1987.

Zupko, Ronald E., and Robert A. Laures. *Straws in the Wind: Medieval Urban Environmental Law—The Case of Northern Italy.* Boulder, CO: Westview Press, 1996.

5. Africa

Anderson, David, and Richard Grove, eds. *Conservation in Africa: People, Policies, and Practice.* Cambridge, UK: Cambridge University Press, 1987.

Beinart, William. "Soil Erosion, Conservationism and Ideas about Development: A Southern African Exploration, 1900–1960." *Journal of Southern African Studies* 11 (1984): 52–83.

Butzer, Karl W. *Early Hydraulic Civilization in Egypt: A Study in Cultural Ecology.* Chicago: University of Chicago Press, 1976.

Carruthers, Jane. *The Kruger National Park: A Social and Political History.* Pietermaritzburg: University of Natal Press, 1995.

Gibson, Clark C. "Killing Animals with Guns and Ballots: The Political Economy of Zambian Wildlife Policy." *Environmental History Review* 19 (1995): 49–75.

Khan, Farieda. "Soil Wars: The Role of the African National Soil Conservation Association in South Africa, 1953–1959." *Environmental History* 2, no. 4 (October 1997): 439–59.

Kjejkshus, H. *Ecology Control and Economic Development in East African History.* Berkeley and Los Angeles: University of California Press, 1977.

Shaw, Brent D. *Environment and Society in Roman North Africa: Studies in History and Archaeology,* and *Rulers, Nomads, and Christians in Roman North Africa.* Aldershot, UK: Variorum, 1995.

6. Australia and the Pacific

Dargavel, John, ed. *Australia's Ever-Changing Forests III: Proceedings of the Third National Conference on Australian Forest History.* Canberra, N.S.W.: Centre for Resource and Environmental Studies, Australian National University, 1997.

Dargavel, John et al., eds. *Changing Tropical Forests: Historical Per-*

spectives on Today's Challenges in Asia, Australasia and Oceania. Canberra, N.S.W.: Australian National University, 1988.

————. *Fashioning Australia's Forests.* Melbourne: Oxford University Press, 1995.

Dovers, Stephen, ed. *Australian Environmental History: Essays and Cases.* Oxford, UK: Oxford University Press, 1994.

Mitchell, Andrew. *A Fragile Paradise: Nature and Man in the Pacific.* London: Collins, 1989.

Powell, J.M. *Environmental Management in Australia, 1788–1914.* Oxford: Oxford University Press, 1976.

Pyne, Stephen J. *Burning Bush: A Fire History of Australia.* New York: Holt, 1991.

7. Latin America

Dean, Warren. *Brazil and the Struggle for Rubber: A Study in Environmental History.* New York: Cambridge University Press, 1987.

————. *With Broadax and Firebrand: The Destruction of the Brazilian Atlantic Forest.* Berkeley and Los Angeles: University of California Press, 1995.

Hecht, Susanna, and Alexander Cockburn. *The Fate of the Forest: Developers, Destroyers and Defenders of the Amazon.* London: Verso, 1989.

Melville, Elinor G.K. *A Plague of Sheep: Environmental Consequences of the Conquest of Mexico.* Cambridge, UK: Cambridge University Press, 1994.

8. North America

Buchholz, C.W. *Rocky Mountain National Park: A History.* Boulder, CO: Associated University Press, 1983.

Carson, Rachel. *Silent Spring.* Boston: Houghton Mifflin, 1962.

Clemmer, Richard O. *Roads in the Sky: The Hopi Indians in a Century of Change.* Boulder, CO: Westview Press, 1995.

Cohen, Michael P. *The Pathless Way: John Muir and American Wilderness.* Madison: University of Wisconsin Press, 1984.

Dunlap, Thomas P. *Saving America's Wildlife.* Princeton: Princeton University Press, 1988.

Egerton, Frank, ed. *History of American Ecology*. New York: Arno, 1977.

Flader, Susan L. *Thinking Like a Mountain: Aldo Leopold and the Evolution of an Ecological Attitude Toward Deer, Wolves, and Forests*. Columbia: University of Missouri Press, 1974.

Golley, Frank Benjamin. *A History of the Ecosystem Concept in Ecology: More Than the Sum of the Parts*. New Haven: Yale University Press, 1993.

Hays, Samuel P. *Conservation and the Gospel of Efficiency: The Progressive Conservation Movement, 1890–1920*. Cambridge: Harvard University Press, 1959.

———. *Beauty, Health and Permanence: Environmental Politics in the United States, 1955–1985*. Cambridge, UK: Cambridge University Press, 1987.

Hirt, Paul W. *A Conspiracy of Optimism: Management of the National Forests Since World War Two*. Lincoln: University of Nebraska Press, 1994.

Hughes, J. Donald. *In the House of Stone and Light: A Human History of the Grand Canyon*. Grand Canyon: Grand Canyon Natural History Association, 1978; reprinted 1991.

———. *North American Indian Ecology*. El Paso: Texas Western Press, 1996.

Leopold, Aldo. *A Sand County Almanac*. London: Oxford University Press, 1949; reprinted 1970.

Marx, Leo. *The Machine in the Garden: Technology and the Pastoral Ideal in America*. New York: Oxford University Press, 1964.

Melosi, Martin V. *Coping with Abundance: Energy and Environment in Industrial America*. New York: Knopf, 1985.

———. "Energy and Environment in the United States: The Era of Fossil Fuels." *Environmental (History) Review* 11 (Fall 1987): 167–68.

———. *Garbage in the Cities: Refuse, Reform and the Environment, 1880–1980*. College Station: Texas A&M Press, 1988.

Merchant, Carolyn. *The Death of Nature: Women, Ecology and the Scientific Revolution*. San Francisco: Harper and Row, 1980.

———. *Radical Ecology: The Search for a Livable World*. New York: Routledge, 1992.

Miller, Char, and Hal K. Rothman, eds. *Out of the Woods: Essays in Environmental History*. Pittsburgh: University of Pittsburgh Press, 1997.

Nash, Roderick. *Wilderness and the American Mind.* 3rd ed. New Haven: Yale University Press, 1982.

Opie, John. *Nature's Nation: An Environmental History of the United States.* Fort Worth, TX: Harcourt Brace, 1998.

Petulla, Joseph M. *American Environmental History.* 2nd ed. Columbus, OH: Merrill, 1988.

Pisani, Donald J. *Water, Land and Law in the West: The Limits of Public Policy, 1850–1920.* Lawrence: University Press of Kansas, 1996.

Pyne, Stephen J. *Fire in America: A Cultural History of Wildland and Rural Fire.* Princeton: Princeton University Press, 1982.

Reisner, Marc. *Cadillac Desert: The American West and Its Disappearing Water.* New York: Penguin Books, 1993.

Rothman, Hal K. *On Rims and Ridges: The Los Alamos Area Since 1880.* Lincoln: University of Nebraska Press, 1992.

Schrepfer, Susan R. *The Fight to Save the Redwoods: A History of Environmental Reform, 1917–1978.* Madison: University of Wisconsin Press, 1983.

Strong, Douglas H. *The Conservationists.* Menlo Park, CA: Addison-Wesley, 1971.

Szasz, Andrew. *EcoPopulism: Toxic Waste and the Movement for Environmental Justice.* Minneapolis: University of Minnesota Press, 1994.

Udall, Stewart. *The Quiet Crisis and the Next Generation.* Salt Lake City: Peregrine Smith, 1988.

Vecsey, Christopher, and Robert Venables, eds. *American Indian Environments: Ecological Issues in Native American History.* Syracuse: Syracuse University Press, 1980.

Worster, Donald. *Rivers of Empire: Water, Aridity and the Growth of the American West.* New York: Pantheon, 1985.

———. *Under Western Skies: Nature and History in the American West.* New York: Oxford University Press, 1992.

Young, John. *Sustaining the Earth: The Story of the Environmental Movement.* Cambridge: Harvard University Press, 1990.

Contributors

Valery J. Cholakov was trained in biological anthropology at the University of Sofia. Later he worked as a historian of science at the Bulgarian Academy of Sciences. At Northwestern University he did a study on the environmental history of Russia. At present, he is a researcher in the Department of History at the University of Illinois, Urbana. Among his publications are *The Nobel Prizes: Men and Discoveries* (Moscow, 1986) and "The Tides of Environmental Discourse," *Science Studies* 7, no. 1 (1994).

J. Donald Hughes is John Evans Professor of History at the University of Denver. He received his Ph.D. from Boston University. He is a founding member of the American Society for Environmental History and former editor-in-chief of *Environmental Review* (now *Environmental History*). His published books include *Pan's Travail:*

Environmental Problems of the Ancient Greeks and Romans (1994, 1996) and *North American Indian Ecology* (1996). He is presently finishing *The Environmental History of the World: Humankind's Changing Role in the Community of Life.*

Diane M. Jones has a Ph.D. in comparative world history from the University of Wisconsin at Madison. She is a part-time teacher of Asian history at Boise State University in Boise, Idaho.

John R. McNeill received his Ph.D. in 1981 from Duke University and since 1985 has taught history at Georgetown University. He has held two Fulbright awards, a Woodrow Wilson Center Fellowship, and a Guggenheim Fellowship, and is the author of about thirty scholarly articles. His recent books include *The Mountains of the Mediterranean World: An Environmental History* (1992) and a forthcoming environmental history of the world in the twentieth century, to appear in 1999.

Martin V. Melosi is Professor of History and Director of the Institute for Public History at the University of Houston. He is past president of the American Society for Environmental History, the National Council on Public History, and the Public Works Historical Society. His major research interests include urban environmental history, the history of technology, public policy history, and comparative environmental history. He has written several books and articles in these areas, including *Creating the Sanitary City: Urban America from colonial Times to the 1990s,* to be published in 1999.

Helen Wheatley is an independent scholar residing in Seattle, Washington. A world comparative historian, she specializes in putting modern U.S. environmental history in a global perspective. She edited a volume, *Agriculture, Resource Exploitation, and Environmental Change,* for the series *An Expanding World* (1997). She served as a member of the faculty for the 1998 NEH Summer Institute on the Environment and World History, 1500–2000. Her current projects include world comparative histories of the fur trade and of nuclear waste management.

Index